How to Prepare For the STATE STANDARDS

VOL. 1

5th Grade Edition

By Robert Berger

carney
EDUCATIONAL SERVICES

CARNEY EDUCATIONAL SERVICES
Helping Students Help Themselves

Special thanks to Rim Namkoong, our illustrator

This book is dedicated to:

The moms and dads who get up early and stay up late. You are the true heroes, saving our future, one precious child at a time.

All the kids who don't make the evening news. To the wide-eyed children, full of love, energy, and wonder. You are as close to perfection as this world will ever see.

TABLE OF CONTENTS

An Overview of Standardized Tests

How Your Child Can Improve Their Score on Standardized Tests

LANGUAGE ARTS

MATH

SOCIAL STUDIES

SCIENCE

An Overview of the Standardized Test

In the spring of 2005, almost all American public school students in grades 2 through 11 took a standardized test as part of each state's standardized testing system. This included non-English speaking children and most children who are in special-education programs. The purpose behind this test is to provide both the school districts and parents with information about how their children are performing compared with other children from across the country. Keep in mind that this is a test of basic skills. The test was written to assess the abilities of students only in specified areas of the curriculum. Each state test is a standardized test. This means that ALL children across the state take the same tests in the same way. The directions given by teachers are the same, as are the amounts of time given to complete each testing section.

Why do schools give this type of test?

The standardized tests tell schools how well they are teaching basic skills which all students need to be successful in the future. Schools receive data about how their students did individually and by grade level. They use this information to help make teaching decisions. For example, if students at the fourth grade level all did well in the spelling section of the test, but didn't do as well in the reading comprehension section, those teachers may want to change the emphasis of their language arts program. Standardized tests are valuable, since they are an objective way to measure how successfully schools are delivering the basis. The idea behind standardizing the test is this: if every child takes the same tests in the same way, then it is a fair way to compare schools and districts. If, for example, one school gave all it's students an extra 5 hours to complete the test, then it would be an unfair advantage given to those children.

Each State Department of Education has taken extraordinary measures to ensure that all children get the same experience when taking the test. All testing materials are to be securely locked in classrooms or administrative offices when testing is not in progress. All teachers are discouraged from discussing test questions. Some districts even have non-teaching school employees act as proctors in classrooms to make sure that the testing procedures were being exactly followed. Schools want objective data about how well they are doing their jobs. Parents want this information as well.

What subject areas do standardized tests seek to measure?

Students in grades 2-8 are tested in two main areas, language arts and math. The specific skills tested within language arts are reading comprehension, spelling, vocabulary, grammar, listening skills and study skills. The math sections of the test measures student mastery of the procedures such as math facts and computations, and then tests their ability to solve applied programs. Each standardized test contains sections that measure student knowledge in science and social studies.

In grades 9 through 11, students were also tested in various reading and math skills. Additionally, these students were tested in science and social studies.

What do my child's standardized scores mean?

In the fall, your child's school should have sent you a copy of his/her scores on the test. Scores for most students were reported on a form that shows National Percentile rankings. For example, if your child received a math problem solving percentile rank of 75, that means that s/he scored better than 75 percent of the national sampling of students at his/her grade level. Student performance on each standardized test is measured by comparing your child's individual scores to scores from a national sample. This sample was created during a 1995 test given to students at various grade levels from across the country. The students selected for this 1995 test were representative of all students in the country. Their scores created a set of "norm scores". Scores of all other students taking each standardized test can be compared against this set of scores. If your child got a percentile rank of 89 in spelling, they scored higher than 89 percent of the national sample. Obviously, this means your child ranks in the top 11 percent of students in the spelling section of the standardized test. A percentile rank of 50 would place your child in the middle of the national sample. As you can see, schools want to ensure that parents get scores that accurately reflect their child's abilities, rather than coaching given by school personnel. In this system, it is important that all students compete on a level playing field.

How valid are my child's standardized test scores?

This is where the controversy begins. Critics of standardized tests point to the inclusion of non-English speaking students in the standardized testing to make the case that results may not be reflective of a child's true abilities in the classroom. For example, if a Spanish-speaking child scores in the 15th percentile in study skills, it may be because s/he simply didn't understand the questions. Thus, his/her score is much lower than it would have been if s/he took the test in Spanish. Another undeniable fact about the standardized tests results was this: children from wealthier suburban school districts performed much better on the test than did children from inner city school districts. Critics of the test contend that wealthier schools in the suburbs have many advantages such as computers or after-school programs which could ultimately help their students' scores on any testing program.

Even with all of this controversy, though, it is still clear that the standardized tests results do tell us a lot about how well children have learned the basic information which schools are supposed to teach. Looking at your child's scores can tell you about their strengths and weaknesses in each of the subject areas tested. Since each Department of Education is committed to continuing standardized tests, you should use your child's current scores as a starting point for the future., You can, and should, assist your child in preparing to take the standardized test in 2005 and beyond. Certainly, the schools and teachers in your state are primarily responsible for preparing your child for this test. Yet, parents have an important role to play. This book will give you some valuable tools you can use in helping your child do their best on this very important standardized test. It is the job of the nations schools to teach the material presented on the standardized test, but your role as a reinforcer of skills and a supporter of your child's progress in school cannot be ignored.

How Your Child Can Improve Their Score On ANY Multiple Choice Standardized Test

Your child has entered an educational world that is run by standardized tests. Students take the Scholastic Aptitude Test (SAT) to help them get into college and the Graduate Record Examination (GRE) to help them get into graduate school. Other exams like the ACT and the PSAT are less famous, but also very important to your child's future success. Schools spend a great deal of time teaching children the material they need to know to do well on these tests, but very little time teaching children HOW to take these tests. This is a gap that parents can easily fill. To begin with, you can look for opportunities to strengthen your child's reading and vocabulary skills as well as their ability to follow detailed written directions.

The importance of reading:

Students who do well on standardized tests tend to be excellent readers. They read for pleasure frequently and have a good understanding of what they have read. You can help support your child as a reader by helping them set aside a regular time to read each and every day. As you may know, children tend to be successful when they follow an established pattern of behavior. Even 15-20 minutes spent reading a magazine or newspaper before bedtime will help. Children should read both fiction and non-fictional material at home, as well as at school. Ask your child about what they have read. Help them to make connections between a book they are currently reading and a movie or a television show they have recently seen. THE BOTTOM LINE: Children who read well will do better on standardized tests then children who do not. There is written material in all sections of the test that much be quickly comprehended. Even the math sections have written information contained in each question.

The importance of building a larger vocabulary:

As you may know, children who read well and who read often tend to have a large vocabulary. This is important since there is an entire section on all standardized tests that is devoted exclusively to the use of vocabulary words. You can support your child in attempting to improve their vocabulary by encouraging them to read challenging material on a regular basis. The newspaper is a good place to start. Studies have shown that many newspaper articles are written on a 4th to 5th grade reading level! Help your child to use new and more difficult words both in their own conversations and in their writings. If you use an advanced vocabulary when speaking to your child, don't be surprised if they begin to incorporate some of the new words into their daily speech. To be honest, one of the most immediate ways to judge the intelligence of anyone is in their use of language. Children are aware of this too. THE BOTTOM LINE: Children who have an expansive vocabulary will do better on any standardized test than children who do not. Find as many ways as possible to help build new words into your child's speech and writing.

The importance of following written directions:

Each state standards test is a teacher-directed test. Teachers tell students how to complete each section of the test, and give them specific examples that are designed to help them understand what to do. However, teachers are not allowed to help students once each test has begun. The written script for teachers seems to repeat one phrase continually: "READ THE DIRECTIONS CAREFULLY". This is certainly not an accident. Students face a series of questions that cannot be answered correctly unless the student clearly understands what is being asked for. Help your child by giving them a series of tasks to complete at home in writing. Directions should be multi-step and should be as detailed as possible without frustrating your child. For example: "Please take out the trash cans this afternoon. Place all the bottles and cans in the blue recycling bin and place all the extra newspapers that are stacked in the garage in the yellow recycling bin." If children are able to follow these types of directions and are able to reread to clarify what is being asked, they will be at a tremendous advantage when it comes to the standardized test. THE BOTTOM LINE: Children who are able to follow a series of detailed, written directions will have a tremendous advantage over those who are unable to do so.

All of the previous suggestions are designed to be used before the test is actually given to help your child improve in some basic test-taking skills. Here are some strategies that you can teach your child to use once they are taking the standardized test:

1. SELECT THE BEST ANSWER.

Each standardized test, like many multiple choice tests, isn't designed for children to write their own answers to the questions. They will fill in a bubble by the four answer choices and select the   BEST possible answer. Reading the question carefully is quite important, since the question may contain key words needed to select the correct answer. For example:

The first President of the United States was

a. John Adams
b. James Madison
c. George Washington
d. Thomas Jefferson

The correct answer is, of course, "c". Students would need to read the question carefully and focus on the key work in the question: "first". All of the names listed were Presidents of the United States early in our history, but only choice "c" contains the name of our first President. Looking for key words like "least" or "greater" will help your child to select the best answer from among the choices given.

2. ANSWER THE EASY QUESTIONS FIRST.

Each state standards test contains a series of timed tests. Children who waste time on a difficult question found at the beginning of a test may run out of time before they finish the entire test. A good strategy is to skip anything that seems too difficult to answer immediately. Once your child has answered every "easy" question in the section, they can go back through the test and spend more time working on the more time-consuming questions. If students are given only 30 minutes to answer 25 reading vocabulary questions, they shouldn't spend much more than a minute on each one. Wasting four or even five minutes on one question is not a good idea, since it reduces the amount of time your child will have to work on the rest of the test. Once time runs out, that's it! Any questions left unanswered will be counted wrong when the test is machine scored. Working on the easier questions first will allow your child to make the best use of the allowed time.

3. ELIMINATE ANY UNREASONABLE ANSWER CHOICES.

No matter how intelligent your child is, it is inevitable that they will come to test questions that they find too difficult to answer. In this situation, the best thing to do is to make an "educated guess". If students can eliminate one or more of the answer choices given, they have a much greater chance of answering the question correctly.

For example:
Select the word below that means the same as the underlined word:

Jennifer became <u>enraged</u> when she found out her diary had been read.

    a. mournful
    b. furious
    c. pleased
    d. depressed

Even if your child didn't know that "b" is the best answer choice, they could certainly eliminate choice "c" from consideration. Clearly, Jennifer would not be "pleased" to find out her diary had been read.

4. DO MATH QUESTIONS ON PAPER WHEN NECESSARY.

The math sections of each standardized test cause children problems because several of the answer choices seem like they could be correct. The only way to select the best answer choice for some math questions is to do the math calculation on scratch paper. The answer choices given for these questions are written to discourage guessing.

For example:

Eileen has saved $3245 to buy a car. Her aunt gave her another $250 as a gift. How much does she have in all?

    a. $3595
    b. $4495
    c. $3495
    d. $3485

The correct answer is "c", but it is hard to select the correct answer because all of the answer choices seem similar. The best way to determine the correct answer would be to added $3545 and $250 on scratch paper.

If you work with your child with these simple strategies, you will find that they will approach these test with confidence, rather than with anxiety. Teach your child to prepare and then to approach the standardized test with a positive attitude. They should be able to say to themselves; "I know this stuff, I'll do a great job today."

LANGUAGE ARTS

Content Cluster: READING VOCABULARY - SYNONYMS

Objective: To evaluate the child's ability to understand word meanings and to use words in context.

Parent Tip: Synonyms are words that mean the same as other words. Students must be able to understand the meaning of the underlined word and to select the word that means the same thing from among the four choices given. Your child should read all four of the choices given and select the one that best matches the underlined word.

Select the word or group of words that means the same as the underlined word.

EXAMPLE: Angela felt <u>exhausted</u>.

   a. tired
   b. angry
   c. bored
   d. frustrated

The correct answer is "a". Tired is a synonym for the word exhausted.

1. We read a <u>humorous</u> story.

   a. tragic
   b. interesting
   c. funny
   d. fictional

2. I <u>guarantee</u> that you'll get paid.

   a. think
   b. understand
   c. guess
   d. promise

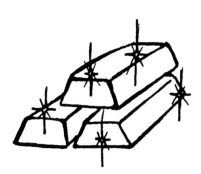

3. She <u>hesitated</u> before crossing the bridge.

   a. wondered
   b. walked
   c. paused
   d. stared

4. The teacher <u>modified</u> the test.
    a. changed
    b. ignored
    c. canceled
    d. removed

5. Billy felt <u>resentful</u>.
    a. satisfied
    b. jealous
    c. peaceful
    d. embarrassed

6. The students were <u>perplexed</u> by the exam.
    a. amused
    b. confused
    c. agitated
    d. depressed

7. Molly looked <u>stunning</u> in her new outfit.
    a. tragic
    b. forlorn
    c. beautiful
    d. hapless

8. Her statement to Aunt Diane was <u>outrageous</u>.
    a. serious
    b. thoughtful
    c. confusing
    d. ridiculous

9. We all loved Mr. Gordo because of his <u>subtle</u> humor.
    a. silly
    b. pointless
    c. deft
    d. sarcastic

10. The firemen in our town showed their <u>boundless</u> courage.
    a. limited
    b. conditional
    c. limitless
    d. occasional

Objective: To evaluate the child's ability to understand word meanings and to use the words in context.

Parent Tip: An antonym is a word that means the opposite of another word. For example, an antonym for the word "delighted" would be "furious." Students must be able to understand the meaning of the underlined word and to select the word that means the opposite from among the four choices given. Your child should read all four of the choices given and select the one that best matches the underlined word.

Select the word or group of words that means the opposite of the underlined word.

EXAMPLE: Jonathan was <u>bored</u>.

a. disinterested
b. unhappy
c. fascinated
d. confused

The correct answer is "c". Fascinated is an antonym for the word bored.

1. The test was quite <u>challenging</u>.

   a. difficult
   b. impossible
   c. simplistic
   d. convoluted

2. Our friends were <u>grieving</u> the death of their neighbor.

   a. mourning
   b. celebrating
   c. sad about
   d. upset about

3. Aunt Aggie has a <u>monstrous</u> temper.

    a. very bad
    b. terrible
    c. pleasant
    d. awful

4. The dog looked <u>forlorn</u> walking down the street.

    a. abandoned
    b. alone
    c. cheerful
    d. saddened

5. Your father's jokes are <u>hilarious</u>.

    a. riotous
    b. tragic
    c. outrageous
    d. quite funny

6. General George Washington played a <u>monumental</u> role in our early history.

    a. insignificant
    b. important
    c. hey
    d. pivotal

7. The small girl seemed quite <u>meek</u>.

    a. harmless
    b. quiet
    c. sensitive
    d. fierce

8. Jennifer was <u>perplexed</u> by the road map.

    a. puzzled
    b. unbothered
    c. confused
    d. baffled

9. The party had a very <u>festive</u> atmosphere.

    a. celebratory
    b. upbeat
    c. mournful
    d. lively

10. Joey had lost interest in the <u>monotonous</u> lesson.

    a. boring
    b. unending
    c. fascinating
    d. repetitive

11. Being called to the front of the class made Manuel feel <u>awkward</u>.

    a. comfortable
    b. bored
    c. young
    d. uneasy

12. Mrs. Smith was pleased with my <u>accurate</u> answer.

    a. honest
    b. detailed
    c. correct
    d. wrong

13. The garage was being <u>converted</u> into another bedroom.

    a. changed
    b. qualified
    c. removed
    d. maintained

14. The wall was made of a <u>flimsy</u> material.

    a. strong
    b. weak
    c. inexpensive
    d. costly

Content Cluster: READING VOCABULARY –
MULTIPLE WORD MEANINGS

Objective: To evaluate word choice in multiple meaning situations.

Parent Tip: Students will encounter questions in the vocabulary section of the test that require them to determine which meaning of a given word is the correct one. Your child will need to read the sentence in the question very carefully and will need to select the answer choice in which the underlined word is used in the same way.

Read the sentences carefully. Select the answer in which the underlined word means the same thing as in the sentence above.

EXAMPLE: We have a dinner <u>reservation</u> for 7:00 p.m.

    a. Jane visited an Indian <u>reservation</u> Nevada.
    b. Mom felt a sense of <u>reservation</u> as she walked into the darkened room.
    c. Our hotel <u>reservation</u> was for March 26th.
    d. Our stay at the Navajo <u>reservation</u> was fun.

The correct answer is "c". In this case, the word "reservation" means reserving a table in a restaurant or reserving a room in a hotel.

1. Please <u>lock</u> the door before you leave.

    a. The ship went through the <u>lock</u> of the canal.
    b. We kept a <u>lock</u> of the baby's hair.
    c. I think you should <u>lock</u> up your bicycle.
    d. Please buy a new <u>lock</u> at the hardware store.

2. The <u>major</u> reason we went to Hawaii was to go surfing.

    a. He was a pitcher in the <u>major</u> leagues.
    b. Carol is the new drum <u>major</u> in the band.
    c. My brother will <u>major</u> in business at his college.
    d. The discovery of fire was a <u>major</u> achievement for mankind.

3. I think I have the <u>right</u> answer.

    a. Jimmy is <u>right</u> handed.
    b. It is the <u>right</u> of all Americans to be free.
    c. I know you will chose the <u>right</u> gift for Mom.
    d. She sat down <u>right</u> next to me.

4. There were a <u>number</u> of people outside yesterday.

    a. Please remember my phone <u>number</u>.
    b. When the band plays the next <u>number</u>, please dance!
    c. Ben Franklin invented a <u>number</u> of things.
    d. Please <u>number</u> your paper on the left side.

5. Donald struggled to keep the math equation in his <u>mind</u>.

    a. Please <u>mind</u> your manners outside.
    b. You will do well in school because you possess a great <u>mind</u>.
    c. Do you <u>mind</u> if I cut ahead of you in line?
    d. Thanks for volunteering to <u>mind</u> Whiskers while I'm away.

6. We decided that we needed to <u>study</u> for the test.

    a. Please <u>study</u> the room so you can tell if anything was taken.
    b. We read a major University <u>study</u> about the human heart.
    c. The teacher told us to <u>study</u> our vocabulary words every night.
    d. When I go into an unfamiliar place, I try to <u>study</u> the surroundings.

7. The boy did a <u>superior</u> job of playing the violin.

    a. We don't like Mary because she acts so <u>superior</u> to us.
    b. Next year, we will take a boat ride on Lake <u>Superior</u>.
    c. Harvard University accepts students with <u>superior</u> grades.
    d. Mark was taught to always be respectful of those whose age was <u>superior</u> to his.

8. Grandma was so special because she was so <u>understanding</u>.

    a. When I traveled to Italy, I had a hard time <u>understanding</u> what was said to me.
    b. Are you <u>understanding</u> how to do this math problem?
    c. Mary and I have an <u>understanding</u> that we will not tease each other on the playground.
    d. Mr. Jenkins was not a very <u>understanding</u> person.

9. That waiter told stories all night long. What a <u>character</u>!

    a. The novel she read contained a fictional <u>character</u>.
    b. Andrew received a citizenship award for his good <u>character</u>.
    c. Could you believe what that <u>character</u> outside the movie theater was doing to get our attention?
    d. Many people believe that a person's <u>character</u> is really created by times of crisis.

10. Anna and I sometimes <u>wear</u> each other's clothes.

    a. Changing your car's motor oil will reduce engine <u>wear</u>.
    b. The long nights working on his book started to <u>wear</u> Tom down.
    c. If I'm going to buy you a shirt, I'll need to know what size you <u>wear</u>.
    d. Answering the same questions began to <u>wear</u> Miss Smith out.

Read each sentence and choose the correct answer.

11. Sharon made a <u>table</u> to compare prices.

    a. piece of furniture
    b. large sign
    c. chart
    d. menu

12. The bridge was too <u>narrow</u> for the big truck to cross.

    a. not long
    b. not wide
    c. old
    d. flimsy

13. A warm winter made the population of rabbits <u>multiply</u>.

    a. increase
    b. move away
    c. decrease
    d. migrate

14. We admired John for standing up for his <u>principles</u> on the playground.

    a. values
    b. school leaders
    c. parents
    d. other students

Content Cluster: READING VOCABULARY –
USING WORDS IN CONTEXT

Objective: To evaluate knowledge of word choice and meaning.

Parent Tip: Your child will need to know how to use words in context. Students must read the sentence carefully and select the best word to complete the statement. In each sentence there are words that give clues to help your child find the correct answer. Discuss these context clues with your child and help them locate this information in each sentence.

Read each statement very carefully. Each statement contains one missing word. Read the four possible choices after the statement and select the best word to complete it.

EXAMPLE: Tina was very tired after going jogging.
She announced to her mother, "I can _____ keep my eyes open."

    a. easily
    b. hardly
    c. always
    d. certainly

The correct answer here is "b". If Tina were tired after jogging, it would be difficult, rather than easy, to stay awake.

1. Toni was having a hard time with her math test. She finally yelled in frustration, "These problems are _____ for me."

    a. simplistic
    b. captivating
    c. impossible
    d. thrilling

2. Shelia announced that she would one day be President of the United States, but her classmates thought this goal was too _____.

    a. uninteresting
    b. unimaginative
    c. unimpressive
    d. unrealistic

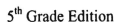

3. The man always seemed to be helping others in times of trouble.
   We were quite impressed by his _____.

   a. solitude
   b. compassion
   c. disinterest
   d. selfishness

4. The television show was very funny.
   The comedian did a dance that was _____.

   a. hilarious
   b. graceful
   c. adept
   d. stirring

5. The food in the restaurant was the best we had ever tasted.
   Matt exclaimed, "This is _____ food."

   a. horrible
   b. disgraceful
   c. nauseating
   d. delicious

6. The new boy wasn't interested in making new friends.
   To us, he seemed to be quite _____.

   a. friendly
   b. solitary
   c. outgoing
   d. extroverted

7. The television program on whales was quite interesting.
   We were _____ by what we learned.

   a. unmoved
   b. bored
   c. confused
   d. fascinated

8. The children in that family were constantly fighting.
There was very little _____ in the family.

    a. conflict
    b. harmony
    c. aggression
    d. anger

9. Because we wanted everyone we knew to see the play that we loved,
we were very _____ in our comments about it.

    a. guarded
    b. enthusiastic
    c. careful
    d. dishonest

10. The atmosphere in our church was quiet and calm.
A feeling of _____ filled the sanctuary as we sat.

    a. serenity
    b. tension
    c. terror
    d. aggression

Content Cluster: READING COMPREHENSION

Objective: To evaluate reading skills using a variety of materials.

Parent Tip: This section will test your child's ability to read and understand both fictional and non-fictional material in a timed situation. The questions after each written passage are challenging! To answer them correctly, your child should be a fairly strong reader with a good comprehension level. Since this is a timed test, students will need to answer as many of the questions as possible from memory. There will be a few questions, however, that cannot be answered successfully without going back and rereading parts of the passage. Students should answer all the questions they can without rereading first. Then, they should go back and reread the entire passage again and try to answer any questions they had to skip. Using these strategies will ensure that your children will make the best use of their time and will thus do better on the reading comprehension section.

Carefully read each passage and the questions that follow it. Select the answer you think is best for each question.

EXAMPLE:

The President of the United States is the leader of our government. His job is to make decisions about how our tax dollars should be spent, both here in America and overseas. Each January, the President must make a speech to Congress in which he outlines his plans for helping the American people during the upcoming year.

A good title for this passage might be:

    a. The Importance of Taxes
    b. The Responsibilities of our President
    c. Why Presidents speak in January
    d. Being President is Easy!

The correct answer is "b" because it captures the essence of the passage.

LATE AGAIN!!

The alarm bell rang at 7:22 a.m. with the piercing squeal of unidentifiable music. Adam staggered to the clock and in one motion, slammed his left hand toward the "off" switch and collapsed back into bed. Soon, he was racing a Formula One turbo car in the Indianapolis 500. He was leading a silver Chevy and just about to cross the finish line when he awoke with a jolt. A look of pure horror came to his face as he raised his head off the pillow and came once again in contact with the alarm clock. It was now 9:18 a.m. "Oh, no" he thought to himself. School had started an hour ago, and he was late again. Why hadn't he gotten up by himself, he wondered? Why hadn't Mrs. Smather awakened him at 7:30 a.m. as she usually did? Why did it have to be Friday that he chose to be lazy and careless and LATE? Today, after all, was the day of the Science Fair. If Mr. Bartholomew caught him walking into school late again today, he would NEVER allow Adam to enter his Recycled Chewing-Gum Engine in the contest.

Adam tried to shake these dreadful theories from his brain as he clumsily put on his pants and shirt. As he raced towards the bathroom, he noticed that his blonde hair was sticking up straight out of his head as if he were the Bride of Frankenstein or that old scientist guy with the white hair who invented the Atom Bomb. Oh well! He hoped that people wouldn't notice. He struggled to get his pants and shirt on and hurriedly ran out the door. He raced toward school, turning his leisurely walk into a frantic run. As he finally reached the front door of the William Mc Kinley School, he got the eerie sensation that something was wrong.

The school parking lot, usually filled with cars, was empty. As he rushed up the steps to open the door, he noticed that the hallways were unusually dark and silent. He tried to open the door, but it was locked securely shut. He started to bang loudly on the door, but nothing happened. No one came to help him. No one cared. He was now utterly and completely alone in the world. Why hadn't he gotten up on time? Why was he so lazy? Why was he so irresponsible? Adam began to wallow in an ever-expanding sea of self-pity. A small tear appeared in his eye.

Soon tears began to flood his eyes. As he lifted his right hand to shield his shameful expression from the outside world, he noticed a very peculiar thing had happened to his watch. It was stuck! He was now frozen in time at 9:55 a.m. in front of an empty school with no one to care for him. Perhaps he had broken the watch during his incessant pounding on the front door. He pressed the button once to check the date setting on the watch. It still worked! Excitedly, he stared at the watch to see the day and date through his tears. Suddenly a feeling of terror unlike anything he had felt previously gripped him. He looked at the watch carefully, convinced that someone had played some kind of terrible joke upon him. His exhausted mind seized upon the one word that had caused him such distress. He looked once more at the watch, convinced that his brain was playing tricks on him. But it was true. It was no trick or illusion. The word appeared again and again on the watch as he pressed the button: SATURDAY!!!!

1. What dream did Adam have after he turned off his alarm?

    a. He was trapped outside the school.
    b. He was a champion race-car driver.
    c. He couldn't get out of bed.
    d. He couldn't enter the Science Fair.

2. Why did seeing the word "Saturday" on his watch upset Adam so much?

    a. It meant his watch really was broken.
    b. It meant that he was late for the Science Fair.
    c. It meant that school had already ended.
    d. It meant that he had run to school on the weekend.

3. Based on the author's description, who is Mr. Bartholomew?

    a. the school's principal
    b. Adam's father
    c. the maker of Adam's watch
    d. an important scientist

4. Why was Adam unhappy when he looked in the mirror?

    a. He thought he looked ugly.
    b. He looked like the Bride of Frankenstein.
    c. He knew he didn't have time to shower.
    d. His hair was sticking up.

5. Which one of these words is not used in the story to describe Adam's feelings about his actions?

    a. ridiculous
    b. lazy
    c. careless
    d. irresponsible

6. How did Adam come to first notice his watch?

    a. He raised his hand to cover his face.
    b. He noticed it had stopped because he had banged on the front door.
    c. He noticed that the watch was stuck at 9:55.
    d. The story doesn't say.

7. According to the story, who is Mrs. Smather?

   a. Adam's Aunt
   b. Adams mother
   c. Adam's housekeeper
   d. The story doesn't say.

8. The author used the word "incessant" to describe the way Adam pounded on the door. A synonym for this word would be:

   a. loud
   b. unending
   c. disturbing
   d. forceful

9. Why do you think the author chose to write the word "Saturday" in capital letters in the story?

   a. It's the last word in the story.
   b. It proved that Adam's watch wasn't broken.
   c. It emphasized Adam's anger about the situation.
   d. The story doesn't say.

10. If Adam learned a lesson from this experience, what do you think it was?

   a. Never be late for school.
   b. Think carefully before you act.
   c. Pay close attention to your surroundings.
   d. Do exactly what important adults say.

SUSAN GERALD FOR CHAIRMAN

October 13th, 1998

Dear Fellow Students:

Hello! My name is Susan Gerald, and I am a sixth grader here at Asco Street Elementary School. As you probably know, I am running for the office of Student Chairman of our School Congress. Ordinarily, you would see posters with my face on them throughout the school, or you would receive a sticker with my name on it to put on your shirt. I have decided to run a different kind of campaign this year. Instead of creating a larger trash problem throughout the school, I have decided to write a letter to each of you explaining why I am running for Chairman. I checked with Miss Malo to see if this broke any school rules, and she said that it didn't. Here are a few ways that I feel that I can help you if you elect me:

1. I will sell candy and soda after school to help us raise money for new playground equipment. We need new soccer balls and another kick ball court. All the profits we make on the snacks will go towards this project.
2. Do you hate to go back to school on Mondays? I do. If you elect me, I'll try to change our release time on Mondays from 3:10 to 12:30! Just think, more time to play outside or be with friends instead of inside your classroom.
3. Are you bored at lunchtime? If you elect me, Miss Malo, our Principal, will have to tap dance and do back flips during lunch recess. I'll also ask her to do cartwheels and handstands in the cafeteria. This will make school much more fun, don't you think?
4. Are you tired of having dogs removed from the school campus by our custodians? If you elect me, I will make it illegal to remove any animal from the school grounds. I think we can learn more if dogs, cats, and other live animals are in the classrooms with us. Our school should be for pets, too.

I think these changes will make our school much more fun and will help everyone learn more. I think these changes will be very easy to make. I have more ideas that I would love to share with you. Please consider voting for me, Susan Gerald, for Student Chairman.

Thank You!!

1. Why did Susan write this letter instead of campaigning in the usual way?

    a. The principal gave her permission.
    b. She wanted to reduce the litter at the school.
    c. She was too lazy to make posters.
    d. The letter doesn't say why.

2. Why does Susan want to sell food after school?

    a. She wants to raise money for equipment.
    b. She wants to raise money to help animals.
    c. She wants to raise money to hire more staff.
    d. She doesn't say why in her letter.

3. Miss Malo will not have to do which of the following at recess if Susan is elected?

    a. tap dance
    b. do back flips
    c. stand on her head
    d. sing

4. Why does Susan think it is a good idea to have dogs at the school?

    a. It's mean to remove them.
    b. The pets will learn more at school.
    c. Students will learn more.
    d. It is illegal to remove them from school.

5. If Susan gets elected, she might have difficulty because:

    a. She might not raise enough money.
    b. Many of her ideas are unrealistic.
    c. Miss Malo cannot do gymnastics.
    d. Dogs may get injured at the school.

6. How does Susan want to change school on Mondays?

    a. She wants to sell food after school.
    b. She wants to end school at 12:30.
    c. She wants to cancel school on Mondays.
    d. She wants to bring pets on campus on Mondays.

7. Which of these statements is true about Susan?

    a. She will say anything to get elected.
    b. She won't be able to do any of her suggestions.
    c. She cares more about entertaining students than learning anything.
    d. She thinks her ideas will be easy to implement.

8. Which statement is true about Susan's ideas?

    a. She doesn't understand that the principal can't dance.
    b. She doesn't understand that one student cannot unilaterally make drastic changes at a school.
    c. She will never be able to raise enough money for the playground.
    d. She doesn't know that animals interfere with learning at school.

9. What advice would you give Susan?

    a. Stop lying to students to get elected.
    b. Please get some better ideas and you'll get elected.
    c. Ask the principal before sending out a letter.
    d. Have the principal read your letter before sending it out.

10. If you were to change the title of this passage, the best choice would be:

    a. Susan Gerald Always Tells the Truth
    b. How I Want to Change our School
    c. How Dogs and Cats Came to Asco Street
    d. Miss Malo Does Backflips

POTATO PIE RECIPE

This recipe is for a favorite dish called potato pie. It goes well with any dish, especially chicken or beef spare ribs. The pie can serve 3-5 people. Note: this recipe can be doubled to serve larger groups. Use a larger pan.

Ingredients:

3 – 4 large Idaho baking potatoes (Peeled)
2 cloves of garlic
3 teaspoons of butter
4 teaspoons of cooking oil
5 cups of white flour
2 teaspoons of salt
½ teaspoon of pepper

A. Put the potatoes and the garlic in a large saucepan. Cover with water and bring to a boil. Then turn down the heat to simmer the potatoes for 40 minutes.
B. While the potatoes are being heated, heat the butter in a small pan. Add the garlic and cook over a low flame until the garlic is dark brown in color. Cook the garlic for 5 minutes then discard it.
C. Drain the potatoes and set them aside.
D. Preheat the oven to 400°.
E. Heat some of the butter mixture in a large aluminum pan. Cook the potatoes until they are evenly browned.

(recipe is continued on page 137)

1. Which of these directions isn't included in the recipe?

    a. Preheat the oven to 400°.
    b. Drain the potatoes and set aside.
    c. Peel each of the potatoes carefully.
    d. Heat the butter mixture in a pan.

2. This recipe for potato pie goes particularly well with:

    a. any chicken dish
    b. chicken and spare ribs
    c. any beef dish
    d. all meats except fish

3. Which cooking utensil is not included in the recipe?

    a. a large saucepan
    b. a teaspoon
    c. a tablespoon
    d. a garlic press

4. How much garlic is called for in the recipe?

    a. two cloves
    b. two tablespoons
    c. two ounces
    d. two teaspoons

5. According to the recipe, what is the last thing to be done with the garlic?

    a. mash it in with the potatoes
    b. save it and reuse
    c. add it after 30 minutes to the baking potatoes
    d. discard it

6. The ingredients listed but not used in first portion of the recipe include:

    a. pepper
    b. potatoes
    c. garlic
    d. butter

7. The recipe requires that you take the potatoes and "cover with water." What does this mean?

    a. rinse them off with water
    b. fill the pan with water
    c. soak them in water, then drain
    d. fill the sink with water and place them in it

8. Which of these directions is not in the recipe?

    a. add 2 teaspoons of salt to the baking potatoes
    b. preheat the oven to 400°
    c. simmer the potatoes for 40 minutes
    d. heat the butter mixture in a large pan

Content Cluster: SPELLING

Objective: To evaluate spelling skills.

> **Parent Tip:** This section will test your child's ability to recognize misspelled words in phrases and within sets of words. One strategy to use in this section is to have your child say each underlined word or answer choice silently as s/he reads it. Words that look or sound strange or unusual are probably not spelled correctly.

Read each phrase below. One of the underlined words in each set of phrases is not spelled correctly. Find the word that is misspelled.

EXAMPLE:

a. an <u>ancient</u> city
b. your <u>confortable</u> shoes
c. a great <u>celebration</u>
d. my <u>exhausted</u> dog

The correct answer is "b". The word "comfortable" is misspelled as "confortable".

1. a. turn <u>right</u> here
    b. a <u>ridiculous</u> story
    c. the <u>silent</u> girl
    d. your <u>fabulouse</u> smile

2. a. my <u>faithful</u> friend
    b. the <u>yapping</u> dog
    c. my guardian <u>angle</u>
    d. a <u>tragic</u> ending

3. a. your big <u>dicision</u>
    b. her <u>amazing</u> catch
    c. the <u>beautiful</u> dawn
    d. a <u>torrential</u> rain

4. a. a <u>major</u> river
    b. her <u>kindley</u> neighbor
    c. my <u>troublesome</u> problem
    d. the <u>final</u> chapter

5. a. the <u>terrific</u> movie
    b. a <u>tremendous</u> explosion
    c. a <u>tallented</u> actor
    d. the <u>talking</u> animal

6. a. her <u>huge</u> purse
    b. the angry <u>reply</u>
    c. an <u>unknowne</u> neighbor
    d. a <u>fierce</u> windstorm

7. a. your <u>silent</u> expression
    b. the <u>stealty</u> cat
    c. a <u>heroic</u> policeman
    d. the <u>confusing</u> letter

8. a. another <u>lonely</u> day
    b. the <u>final</u> chapter
    c. a <u>faitful</u> friend
    d. this <u>planet</u> Earth

9. a. our <u>dirty</u> floor
    b. the <u>over-sized</u> gift
    c. John's <u>nosiey</u> relatives
    d. Her u<u>nbelievable</u> story

10. a. my <u>repulsive</u> pet
    b   your <u>terribel</u> excuse
    c. Carlos's <u>distant</u> cousin
    d. The <u>overpriced</u> dress

MISSPELLED WORD WITHIN SETS OF WORDS

Look at each set of words below. One of these words is spelled incorrectly. Find the misspelled word.

EXAMPLE: a. terriffied
  b. huge
  c. community
  d. convincing

The correct answer is "a". Terriffied is spelled incorrectly.

1. a. foolish
  b. frequently
  c. friendles
  d. fillet

2. a. employment
  b. entretainment
  c. enthusiastic
  d. envelopes

3. a. suspicious
  b. supersonic
  c. supremacy
  d. submraine

4. a. minutes
  b. minisscule
  c. miners
  d. minuet

5. a. fantastic
  b. fascinnating
  c. fabulous
  d. freezing

6. a. delicious
  b. dumfounded
  c. derivative
  d. downtrodden

7. a. popularity
  b. population
  c. purplexing
  d. purple

8. a. suspicious
   b. suspensful
   c. supersonic
   d. supremacy

9. a. germinate
   b. garbled
   c. guiltless
   d. garbagge

10. a. noticeable
    b. noisy
    c. numbericol
    d. normal

11. a. imagine
    b. imballance
    c. imitate
    d. immaculate

12. a. crystalize
    b. cryptic
    c. cryogenics
    d. crustacean

13. a. jeopardy
    b. jewel
    c. jiterbug
    d. jingle

14. a. protoplasm
    b. protection
    c. protracktor
    d. protest

15. a. thermol
    b. thirteenth
    c. threshold
    d. thorough

Content Cluster: CAPITALIZATION AND PUNCTUATION

Objective: To evaluate knowledge of correct mechanics of writing.

Parent Tip: This section will test your child's ability to distinguish between correct and incorrect capitalization and punctuation in phrases and sentences. It will also test your child's ability to determine errors in word usage. Finally, your child will be asked to determine errors in sentence organization and sentence combination. Your child should read all four choices carefully before deciding which one represents the best answer. Selecting the best possible capitalization or punctuation for a given statement isn't easy. Your child should perhaps read all the choices silently and eliminate answer choices that are clearly wrong or "don't seem right." Remember that the answer choices are written to look very similar to one another to discourage random guessing by the student.

Select the proper way to capitalize the word or words that go in the blank.

EXAMPLE: Mr. Jenkins is from _____.

      a. north carolina
      b. north Carolina
      c. North Carolina
      d. North carolina

The correct answer is "c". Mr. Jenkins is from North Carolina.

1. Chile is located in _____.

      a. South america
      b. South America
      c. south America
      d. south america

2. That book was written by _____.

      a. S.E. hinton
      b. s.e. Hinton
      c. s.E. Hinton
      d. S.E. Hinton

3. Two gas planets in our solar system are _____.

      a. jupiter and saturn
      b. Jupiter And Saturn
      c. jupiter and Saturn
      d. Jupiter and Saturn

4. America's most famous museums are located in _____.

   a. Washington, d.c.
   b. washington D. C.
   c. Washington D. C.
   d. Washington d. C.

5. Our two uncles are named _____.

   a. Stanley and phil
   b. stanley and Phil
   c. Stanley and Phil
   d. stanley and phil

6. Two of California's most populated cities are _____.

   a. San diego and san francisco
   b. San Diego and San francisco
   c. San Diego and san Francisco
   d. San Diego and San Francisco

7. George Bush's official title is _____.

   a. President of the united States
   b. President of the United States
   c. president of the United States
   d. President of the united states

8. Our favorite teachers are _____.

   a. Miss Jones and Mr. Bundy
   b. Miss jones and Mr Bundy
   c. miss Jones and Mr. Bundy
   d. Miss Jones and mr. Bundy

9. Our favorite vacation spots are _____.

   a. Las vegas and yellowStone
   b. Las vegas and YellowStone
   c. Las Vegas and yellowstone
   d. Las Vegas and Yellowstone

10. The most famous museums in the world are located in _____.

    a. paris france
    b. Paris, france
    c. paris, France
    d. Paris, France

11. Our family lives near _____.

    a. seattle, Washington
    b. Seattle Washington
    c. Seattle, washington
    d. Seattle, Washington

12. The leader of our school is named _____.

    a. principal smith
    b. Principal smith
    c. Principal Smith
    d. Principal smith

13. The first two battles of the Revolutionary War happened in _____ in 1775.

    a. lexington and Concord, mass
    b. Lexington and Concord, Mass.
    c. Lexington and concord Mass.
    d. Lexingtion and Concord, Mass

14. My two friends are named _____.

    a. Margaret and Norma jean
    b. margaret And Norma-Jean
    c. Margaret and normaJean
    d. Margaret and Norma-Jean

15. The bombing of Pearl Harbor occurred on _____.

    a. Dec. 7, 1941
    b. Dec. 7 1941
    c. dec. 7, 1941
    d. dec. 7 1941

Read each sentence or question. Find the word or phrase with correct punctuation.

EXAMPLE: We saw _____ on T. V. last night.

    a. Mrs. Solomon, our teacher,
    b. Mrs. Solomon, our teacher
    c. Mrs. Solomon our teacher
    d. Mrs. Solomon: our teacher.

The correct answer is "b".

1. _____ happy about my math score.

    a. Im
    b. Im'
    c. I'm
    d. I'm,

2. To win this _____ we must try hard.

    a. game
    b. game:
    c. game;
    d. game,

3. "Hey," shouted Jackie, _____

    a. "I lost my watch"
    b. "I lost my watch!"
    c. "I lost my watch?"
    d. "I lost my watch,"

4. Which is the correct way to close a letter?

    a. Yours Truly:
    b. Yours Truly.
    c. Yours truly,
    d. Yours truly

5. _____ coming to my house next week.

    a. Your
    b. Youre'
    c. your
    d. You're

6. _____ understand why I got a "C" on that test!

    a. I cant
    b. I Cant
    c. I can't
    d. I Cant'

7. Do you understand how to answer _____

    a. this Question.
    b. this question?
    c. this Question?
    d. this Question!

8. _____ win this game!

    a. were gonna
    b. Were going to
    c. We're gonna
    d. We're going to

9. _____Mrs. Jarvis calmly requested.

    a. "Please feed Fido!"
    b. "please feed Fido?"
    c. "Please feed Fido,"
    d. "Please feed Fido:"

10. _____ said Mom.

    a. "we need eggs milk and Cheese at the store"
    b. "We need eggs milk and cheese at the store"
    c. "We need eggs, milk and cheese, at the store"
    d. "We need eggs, milk, and cheese at the store,"

SELECTING PROPER WORD USAGE

Read each sentence. Look for the word or phrase that completes the sentence correctly.

EXAMPLE:

Mrs. Smith's cat _____.

      a. were meowing
      b. weren't meowing
      c. did meowing
      d. is meowing

The correct answer is "d". Mrs. Smith's cat is meowing.

1. He helped _____ to some dinner.

      a. himselves
      b. himself
      c. him
      d. hisself

2. Joan and _____ went to the movies.

      a. me
      b. us
      c. I
      d. We

3. The ushers _____ people sit down.

      a. were helping
      b. did helped
      c. helps
      d. is helping

4. I will not wear my jacket _____ I need it.

      a. because
      b. before
      c. however,
      d. unless

5. The baseball players _____ around the bases.

    a. running
    b. walks
    c. were running
    d. has refused to run

6. Martha and Aunt Paula _____ a big trip.

    a. plans
    b. are planning
    c. planning
    d. to plan

7. _____ shouted the child.

    a. "Please Help!"
    b. "Helping Please!"
    c. "Helping!"
    d. "Could Help!"

8. _____ said the girl on her birthday.

    a. "Excitement!!"
    b. "You're excited?"
    c. "I'm excited!"
    d. "How excited again?"

9. We _____ for yesterday's test.

    a. studied
    b. will study
    c. to study
    d. study

10. The team _____ play baseball.

    a. loved to
    b. refusing to
    c. thought about
    d. did not want

SELECTING PROPER SENTENCE STRUCTURE

Look for a mistake in the way the sentence is organized. Select the answer choice that shows the best way to rewrite the sentence.

EXAMPLE:

Judy's her friends I am one of.

      a. I am one of her friends.
      b. I am one of Judy's friends.
      c. I am one of Judy's her friends.
      d. I'm one of her friends and so is Judy.

The correct answer is "b". I am one of Judy's friends.

1. The United States President in the White House lives.

      a. The President of the United States lives in the White House.
      b. The President of the United States. Lives in the White House.
      c. The President of the United States is in the White House.
      d. The Presidents of the United States live in the White House.

2. By her every colored pencil was used.

      a. Every colored pencil was used by her.
      b. Every colored pencil was used. By her.
      c. Every colored pencil was used. She used it.
      d. Every colored pencil was hers. She used them.

3. Mount Vernon once a magnificent home, now a museum is.

      a. Once a magnificent home. Mount Vernon is now a museum.
      b. Once a magnificent home, Mount Vernon is now a museum.
      c. Once a magnificent home, Mount Vernon. Is now a museum.
      d. Once a magnificent home: Mount Vernon is now a museum.

4. Very funny we found Mr. Smith to be.

      a. We found Mr. Smith. To be very funny.
      b. We found Mr. Smith, to be very funny.
      c. We found Mr. Smith very funny to be.
      d. We found Mr. Smith to be very funny.

5. Mrs. Wright the school is the principal of.

    a. The school is the principal of Mrs. Wright
    b. Mrs. Wright is the principal of the school.
    c. The principal of is the school Mrs. Wright.
    d. The school Mrs. Wright is the principal of.

6. Lucky Dog Biscuits enjoys our dog Lucy.

    a. Enjoys our dog Lucy Lucky Dog Biscuits.
    b. Dog Biscuits Lucky our dog Lucy enjoys.
    c. Our dog, Lucy, enjoys Lucky Dog Biscuits.
    d. Lucy our dog Lucky Dog Biscuits enjoys.

7. The oldest person I know Grandma Josephine is.

    a. I know the oldest person Grandma Josephine is.
    b. The oldest person Grandma Josephine is I know.
    c. Grandma Josephine is the oldest person I know.
    d. Is I know the oldest person Grandma Josephine.

8. Arizona for our vacation we are going to.

    a. For our vacation, we are going to Arizona.
    b. Going to Arizona we are for our vacation.
    c. Arizona going to for our vacation we are.
    d. Vacation we are for our Arizona going to.

9. Do you know what birthday for you would like Sam?

    a. What birthday do you know Sam for you would like?
    b. Sam, do you know what you would like for your birthday?
    c. You would like for birthday do you know what Sam?
    d. Birthday for you Sam would like what do you know?

10. Do well on the test we will!

    a. We will on the test do well!
    b. Do well we will on the test!
    c. We will do well on the test!
    d. On the test do well we will!

LANGUAGE ARTS
Answer Key

Synonyms

1. c
2. d
3. c
4. a
5. b
6. b
7. c
8. d
9. c
10. c

Antonyms

1. c
2. b
3. c
4. c
5. b
6. a
7. d
8. b
9. c
10. c
11. a
12. d
13. d
14. a

Multiple Meanings

1. c
2. d
3. c
4. c

5. b
6. c
7. c
8. d
9. c
10. c
11. c
12. b
13. a
14. a

Context

1. c
2. d
3. b
4. a
5. d
6. b
7. d
8. b
9. b
10. a

Reading Comprehension

1. b
2. d
3. a
4. d
5. a
6. a
7. d
8. b
9. c

10. b
1. b
2. a
3. d
4. c
5. b
6. b
7. d
8. b
9. d
10. b

1. c
2. b
3. c
4. a
5. d
6. a
7. b
8. a

Spelling

1. d
2. c
3. a
4. b
5. c
6. c
7. b
8. c
9. c
10. b

1. c
2. b

3. d
4. b
5. b
6. b
7. c
8. b
9. d
10. c
11. b
12. a
13. c
14. c
15. a

Capitalization

1. b
2. d
3. d
4. c
5. c
6. d
7. b
8. a
9. d
10. d
11. d
12. c
13. b
14. d
15. a

Punctuation

1. c
2. a
3. b

4. c
5. d
6. c
7. b
8. d
9. c
10. d

Word Usage

1. b
2. c
3. a
4. d
5. c
6. b
7. a
8. c
9. a
10. a

Sentence Structure

1. a
2. a
3. b
4. d
5. b
6. c
7. c
8. a
9. b
10. c

MATH

Content Cluster: PROBLEM SOLVING

Objective: To evaluate knowledge of problem solving strategies that involve multiple-step thinking.

Parent Tip: Your child will be asked to add, subtract, multiply, and divide whole numbers and fractions and apply the operations in context. Most of this section is made up of word problems that must be read, understood, and solved correctly within a very short amount of time. In this section, it is not enough just to be able to compute accurately. The reading and comprehension of the problem is equally important. Make sure your child understands what the problem is asking or which operation to use to solve the problem before he begins to compute.

EXAMPLE:

Joe and Mary collected acorns for five months. At the end of that time, Mary had 3,415 acorns and Joe had 4,296 acorns. How many more acorns did Joe have than Mary?

     a. 880
     b. 881
     c. 882
     d. 884

The correct answer is "b". Joe had 881 more acorns than Mary.

Here are the steps your child should go through to solve this problem quickly and accurately:

1. Carefully read the problem and decide which information is not necessary to solve it. In this problem, the fact that the children have been collecting the acorns for five months is not needed. Thus, your child should focus on the last two sentences of the word problem and ignore the first.
2. Decide which operation to use. In this problem, it is clear form the words "how many more" that your child will need to subtract the number 3,415 from the number 4,296. Train your child to look at the last sentence before the question mark. This will help him/her to quickly identify the math operation to use.
3. Do the math accurately. It is very important that your child is able to do basic equations quickly and accurately. It is also important to point out that calculators and other computation aids cannot be used on this test. Your child would be expected to do this problem on scratch paper.
4. Select the best answer. Once your child has calculated the right answer, s/he can easily select the correct answer from among the four choices given. In the above problem, answer "b" is correct. If your child had guessed or estimated the answer, s/he would not have been able to determine which of the four choices would be correct, because the answer choices are only one or two numbers apart. Only accurate subtraction will reveal the correct answer.

With all of the steps required in this section of the test, it is very important for students to remember to use their time wisely. If any question seems too complicated to be solved in more than a few minutes, your child should skip it and return to it after all of the other problems have been solved. Your child must keep moving through the test section and must not get hung up on one particular problem.

Read each question carefully and find the correct answer.

1. Jacob's mother and father walk about 2.5 miles per day. They walk 7 days each week. How far do they walk each week?

   a. 16.2 miles
   b. 17.5 miles
   c. 17.2 miles
   d. 18.2 miles

2. A car gets 30 miles per gallon of gasoline. About how much gasoline would a family use by driving to San Diego, which is 58 miles away from their home?

   a. 2 gallons
   b. 3 gallons
   c. 4 gallons
   d. 5 gallons

3. If you bought a bag of potato chips for 85 cents and a magazine for $2.25, how much change would you have left over if you paid with a 20-dollar bill?

   a. $15.75
   b. $12.23
   c. $16.68
   d. $16.90

4. Jenny is flying to New York in May. She called her travel agent and found out that a first class ticket will cost her $560.00 and an economy ticket will cost her $341.00. She wants to know how much money she will save if she flies economy. How would you solve this problem?

   a. $560.00 + $341.00
   b. $560.00 - $341.00
   c. ($560.00 + $341.00) – ($560.00 - $341.00)
   d. $560.00 + 560.00 - $341.00

5. At lunchtime, 350 students eat lunch in the cafeteria. Each table can hold 30 students. About how many tables are there?

   a. 11
   b. 13
   c. 14
   d. 20

6. What facts do you need to find the average height of students in your class?

   a. the number of students in your class and their grade level
   b. the number of students and their heights
   c. the height of each student
   d. the height of only the three tallest and three shortest students

A survey was held to determine which foods students at an elementary school liked best. Here are the results:

Pizza 52%
Hamburgers 20%
Hot Dogs 12%
Tacos 10%
Pork Chops 6 %

Using the above statement answer the next two questions.

7. What percentage of students preferred something other than pizza?

   a. 46%
   b. 40%
   c. 48%
   d. 45%

8. When you combine those students who preferred hamburgers and hot dogs together, they are still less than 50% of those students surveyed. If those students who wanted _____ had switched to hamburgers or hot dogs, they would have just over 50%.

   a. pizza
   b. tacos
   c. pork chops
   d. none of the above

9. Which of these equations could be used to divide up a 40-ounce bag of candy among 5 people?

   a. $5 \div 40$
   b. $40 - 5$
   c. $40 + 5$
   d. $40 \div 5$

The table below shows the cost of different sized plastic containers. Use the information in the table to answer the following questions:

10" x 12" x 24" = $3.50
12" x 14" x 24" = $4.50
12" x 12" x 12" = $3.00
14" x 14" x 16" = $3.25
18" x 18" x 30" = $5.00

10. What is the price difference between the most expensive and the least expensive plastic container?

   a. $2.50
   b. $2.00
   c. $3.00
   d. $1.00

11. If you had an object with the dimensions 11" x 13" x 15", what is the cheapest container you could use to put it in?

   a. 12" x 14" x 24"
   b. 12" x 12" x 12"
   c. 14" x 14" x 16"
   d. 18" x 18" x 30"

12. How many of these containers can hold a 17" x 17" x 2" photo album?

   a. 3
   b. 2
   c. 1
   d. 4

13. About how long is this drawing of a pencil? (one inch = 2.54 cm.)

   a. ½ a foot
   b. ½ a yard
   c. 17 centimeters
   d. 1 ½ inches

Centimeters

14. A flight attendant works on two 4-hour flights between Los Angeles and Dallas and then goes home. How much of the day has she worked?

   a. 1/5
   b. 2/3
   c. 1/3
   d. 3/5

15. Which of these is another way to write 4/6?

    a. 6/4
    b. 1/5
    c. 2/3
    d. 12/15

16. Which of these fractions is not equivalent to ½?

    a. 5/10
    b. 9/18
    c. 51/100
    d. 75/150

17. What is 385,007 rounded to the nearest hundred thousand?

    a. 390,000
    b. 400,000
    c. 380,000
    d. 370,000

18. Carl's Computer World has 90 workers. Each worker can assemble 20 computers in an hour. How many computers can the company produce in an eight hour work day?

    a. 15,000
    b. 14,400
    c. 14,500
    d. 14,600

19. $2^4 \times 3 =$

    a. 36
    b. 48
    c. 44
    d. 42

20. $3^2 \times 4 =$

    a. 27
    b. 32
    c. 36
    d. 40

21. 2^2 x 4 x 5 =

    a. 70
    b. 80
    c. 90
    d. 100

22. 8^3 x 6 x 2 =

    a. 6122
    b. 6144
    c. 6126
    d. 6128

23. What is 1285 rounded to the nearest hundred?

    a. 1290
    b. 1200
    c. 1300
    d. 1280

24. What is 745 rounded to the nearest ten?

    a. 750
    b. 740
    c. 700
    d. 800

25. What is 52,687 rounded to the nearest thousand?

    a. 52,000
    b. 52,700
    c. 53,000
    d. 52,600

Content Cluster: MATH PROCEDURES

Objective: To evaluate the use of numbers in various mathematical situations and compute them accurately.

Parent Tip: Your children should be comfortable performing mathematical operations quickly and should be able to check his/her work by using inverse operations. This means that they should be able to check their work in a division problem by using multiplication. Students who can do simple math equations without working them out on paper will be able to save time. It is important to remember that since this is a timed test, students should do the simplest problems first. Problems that require paper and pencil calculation should be done quickly, yet carefully. Finally, students must remember to quickly scan the problem before answering to determine which operation to use. It is very important to watch the signs (+, -, x, ÷) in every problem.

Read each problem carefully and choose the correct answer.

EXAMPLE: 0.5 x 0.7 =

      a. 35
      b. 350
      c. 0.35
      d. 0.035

The correct answer here is "c". Since two decimals are being multiplied, the answer would also have to be a decimal. Thus, answer choices "a" and "b" would be eliminated. A basic understanding of place value would also eliminate choice "d".

1. 720 ÷ 8 =

      a. 9
      b. 19
      c. 90
      d. 900

2. 2 2/8 + 5 5/8 =

      a. 7 7/8
      b. 8
      c. 8 3/8
      d. 9 3/8

3. 412 x 517 =

   a. 210,000
   b. 212,130
   c. 212,330
   d. 213,004

4. $8.29 + $6.31 =

   a. $12.50
   b. $14.60
   c. $14.50
   d. $14.59

5. This new CD is on sale for $12.95. Rounded to the nearest dollar, what is the price?

   a. $12.00
   b. $12.50
   c. $13.00
   d. $13.95

6. Lake Pontoski is 127 feet across at it's widest point. How many inches across is the lake?

   a. 1,522 inches
   b. 1,524 inches
   c. 1,525 inches
   d. 1,530 inches

7. 2/5 x 10/11 =

   a. 1/5
   b. 4/11
   c. 3/5
   d. 1 1/11

8. Jane and Janine decided to add up all the minutes they spent playing video games during the months of October and November. The total came to 389,527 minutes. Round this number to the nearest hundred thousand.

   a. 400,000
   b. 300,000
   c. 390,000
   d. 450,000

9. Which set of numbers is in the same family of facts as: 3 x 8 = _____

    a. _____ x 3 = 8
    b. 8 + 3 = _____
    c. _____ ÷ 8 = 3
    d. 8 - _____ = 3

10. 324,125 – 135,132 =

    a. 188,993
    b. 188,992
    c. 189,993
    d. 189,991

11. A rain gage measured the amount of rainfall in Cooperville over a four-day period. On Monday, 1.5 inches fell. On Tuesday, 2.3 inches fell. On Wednesday, 0.9 of an inch fell. On Thursday, 2.2 inches fell. Which list shows the rainfall from least to most?

    a. Wednesday, Monday, Thursday, Tuesday
    b. Wednesday, Monday, Tuesday, Thursday
    c. Wednesday, Tuesday, Monday, Thursday
    d. Wednesday, Tuesday, Thursday, Monday

12. Use the illustration to decide which statement is true.

    a. 14/20 are not shaded
    b. 7/21 are not shaded
    c. 1/3 are shaded
    d. 2/3 are shaded

13. 382 + 4, 435 + 56, 231 + 7 =

    a. 61, 051
    b. 61, 055
    c. 61, 041
    d. none of the above

14. $5,421 - 3,961 =$

   a. 1445
   b. 1458
   c. 1460
   d. 1463

15. John started yardwork at 12:30 p.m. and finished at 4:15 p.m. How long did he work in the yard?

   a. four hours and ten minutes
   b. three hours and forty-five minutes
   c. three hours and thirty minutes
   d. none of the above

16. $610 \div 10 =$

   a. 60
   b. 61
   c. 6100
   d. 610

17. $474 \div 6 =$

   a. 81
   b. 80
   c. 79
   d. 78

18. $592 \div 8 =$

   a. 72
   b. 74
   c. 76
   d. 78

19. $1022 \div 14 =$

   a. 71
   b. 72
   c. 73
   d. 84

20. $3\ 3/8 - 1\ 1/8 =$

   a. 1 3/8
   b. 2 3/8
   c. 2 1/4
   d. 3 1/8

21. $4\ 1/8 + 3\ 5/8 =$

   a. 7 5/8
   b. 7 3/4
   c. 4 3/4
   d. 3 6/8

22. $711 \times 313 =$

   a. 212,543
   b. 222,543
   c. 213,540
   d. 212,541

23. $633 \times 916 =$

   a. 577,828
   b. 566,828
   c. 579,828
   d. 589,828

24. 117 ÷ 13 =

    a. 6
    b. 7
    c. 8
    d. 9

25. 126 ÷ 14 =

    a. 7
    b. 8
    c. 9
    d. 11

26. 133 ÷ 19 =

    a. 5
    b. 6
    c. 7
    d. 8

27. 192 ÷ 16 =

    a. 11
    b. 12
    c. 13
    d. 14

28. 143 ÷ 13 =

    a. 11
    b. 12
    c. 13
    d. 15

29. 165 ÷ 15 =

    a. 9
    b. 10
    c. 11
    d. 13

30. 156 ÷ 13 =

    a. 6
    b. 8
    c. 12
    d. 14

31. 228 ÷ 19 =

    a. 16
    b. 14
    c. 12
    d. 8

32. 20 x 22 =

    a. 420
    b. 430
    c. 434
    d. 440

33. 31 x 15 =

    a. 401
    b. 465
    c. 461
    d. 460

34. 37 x 13 =

    a. 480
    b. 481
    c. 483
    d. 485

35. 17 x 29 =

    a. 490
    b. 491
    c. 492
    d. 493

Content Cluster: WHOLE NUMBER CONCEPTS

Objective: Students will understand how whole numbers work in various mathematical operations.

> **Parent Tip:** Students need to carefully examine all four choices and select the correct answer choice. Keep in mind that the numbers will be very close to each other to discourage guessing! Finally, students may wish to re-read the question after making their answer selection as a way of double checking their work.

Read each problem carefully and choose the correct answer.

EXAMPLE:

Which of the following is an even number?

    a. 12
    b. 13
    c. 21
    d. 99

The correct answer is "a". 12 is an even number.

1. Which numeral shows fifty-two thousand one hundred twenty five?

    a. 5125
    b. 5225
    c. 52,125
    d. 52,1025

2. What is the value of 4 in 10,430?

    a. 4 thousands
    b. 4 hundreds
    c. 4 tens
    d. 4 ten-thousands

3. Which of the following is a factor of 18?

    a. 17
    b. 12
    c. 9
    d. 7

4. Which of these numbers has the greatest value?

    a. 2510
    b. 2501
    c. 2500
    d. 2511

5. Which of these numbers is a factor of 72?

    a. 7
    b. 42
    c. 8
    d. 13

6. What is the value of 2 in 12,786?

    a. 2 thousands
    b. 2 ten thousands
    c. 2 hundreds
    d. 2 tens

7. Which number is missing?   12, 18, ____, 30

    a. 23
    b. 24
    c. 21
    d. 20

8. Which numeral shows twenty four thousand three hundred seventeen?

    a. 240317
    b. 2317
    c. 24,317
    d. 24,307

9. Which of the following numerals has the LEAST value?

   a. 54,879
   b. 54,798
   c. 54,987
   d. 54,797

10. What is 1238 rounded to the nearest hundred?

   a. 1100
   b. 2000
   c. 1200
   d. 1230

11. What is the value of 8 in 11,685?

   a. 8 ones
   b. 8 tens
   c. 8 hundreds
   d. 8 thousands

12. Which address is an even number?

   a. 351 Oakwood Lane
   b. 507 Oakwood Lane
   c. 733 Oakwood Lane
   d. none of the above

13. What is the missing number in this sequence?

   27, 54, 108, _____, 432

   a. 200
   b. 216
   c. 231
   d. none of the above

14. What is 44,841 rounded to the nearest ten-thousand?

   a. 45,000
   b. 40,000
   c. 46,000
   d. none of the above

Content Cluster: WHOLE NUMBER COMPUTATION

Objective: Students will use whole numbers correctly in addition, subtraction, multiplication, and division.

Parent Tip: Your child should watch the signs carefully to determine which operations to use. Also, s/he should practice solving problems mentally, to save time whenever possible.

Read each problem carefully and choose the correct answer.

EXAMPLE: 323 x 254 =

      a. 82042
      b. 82142
      c. 82242
      d. none of the above

The correct answer is "a". 82,042 is the result of 323 x 254.

1. 279 + 167 =

      a. 444
      b. 446
      c. 448
      d. 445

2. 2500 divided by 5 =

      a. 5000
      b. 50
      c. 500
      d. 5

3. 63 x 75 =

      a. 4700
      b. 4720
      c. 4724
      d. none of the above

4. 12423 − 10013 =

   a. 2410
   b. 2310
   c. 2409
   d. none of the above

5. 600 x 18 =

   a. 10900
   b. 10700
   c. 10800
   d. none of the above

6. 67,897 − 54,908 =

   a. 12,987
   b. 12,989
   c. 12,988
   d. none of the above

7. 250,879 + 964,987 =

   a. 1,215,866
   b. 1,214,866
   c. 1,215,766
   d. none of the above

8. 543 x 22 =

   a. 10,946
   b. 11,936
   c. 11,946
   d. none of the above

9. 22 + 32 + 45 + 18 =

   a. 117
   b. 116
   c. 118
   d. none of the above

10. 12,521 x 21 =

   a. 262,940
   b. 262,941
   c. 262,942
   d. none of the above

11. 976 − 587 =

   a. 390
   b. 389
   c. 386
   d. none of the above

12. 154 + 265 =

   a. 419
   b. 420
   c. 418
   d. 416

13. 1140 divided by 2 equals

   a. 565
   b. 575
   c. 572
   d. none of the above

14. 364 ÷ 7 =

   a. 62
   b. 61
   c. 52
   d. 51

15. 245 + 752 =

   a. 897
   b. 998
   c. 997
   d. 898

Content Cluster: FRACTIONS AND DECIMALS

Objective: Students will understand and utilize fractions and decimals in mathematical operations.

Parent Tip: When comparing fractions with different denominators such as 2/3 and 1/6, students will need to convert them to "like" fractions with the same denominator. When students are comparing decimals such as 2.34 and 23.4, they will need to write the decimals in a column so that the decimal points are lined up with one another.

Read each problem carefully and choose the correct answer.

EXAMPLE: Which fraction is equivalent to 6/10?

    a. 1/6
    b. 3/6
    c. 3/10
    d. 3/5

The correct answer is "d". 3/5 is equivalent to 6/10.

1. Which fraction is equivalent to 8/12?

    a. 1/2
    b. 1/3
    c. 2/3
    d. none of the above.

2. Which amount is greatest?

    a. $1.11
    b. $0.11
    c. $1.01
    d. none of the above

3. Which fraction is equivalent to 8/24?

    a. 1/2
    b. 1/4
    c. 2/6
    d. none of the above

4. Find the sum of 0.3, 1.22, 6.98 and .002

   a. 8.041
   b. 8.502
   c. 8.601
   d. none of the above

5. Johnny ate 2/3 of a gallon of vanilla ice cream.
   Jack ate 5/6 of a gallon of chocolate ice cream.
   Jim ate ½ of a gallon of strawberry ice cream.
   Who ate the most ice cream?

   a. Johnny
   b. Jack
   c. Jim
   d. They ate the same amount

6. Which decimal is the smallest amount?

   a. 0.3
   b. 0.03
   c. 0.003
   d. 0.0003

7. $0.25 is what fraction of a dollar?

   a. 1/5
   b. 1/4
   c. 1/3
   d. 1/2

8. Which decimal is equal to 4/5?

   a. 0.8
   b. 0.6
   c. 0.5
   d. 0.4

9. ½ + ½ + ¼ =

   a. 2 ¼
   b. 1 ¼
   c. 1
   d. none of the above

10. Which fraction equals the smallest amount?

    a. 1/3
    b. 2/4
    c. 11/12
    d. 9/10

11. $6.75 + $8.23 =

    a. $14.97
    b. $15.00
    c. $14.99
    d. $14.98

12. 8/9 – 2/9 =

    a. 3/2
    b. 2/3
    c. 3/5
    d. 5/9

13. 2 2/8 + 5 5/8 =

    a. 8
    b. 7 1/8
    c. 7 7/8
    d. 8 7/8

14. 0.3 x 0.6 =

    a. 0.9
    b. 0.3
    c. 1
    d. none of the above

15. 4.08 + 6.89 + 9.99 + 8.76 + 4.49 + 3.99 + 6.99 =

    a. 45.19
    b. 46.18
    c. 45.18
    d. none of the above

Content Cluster: GEOMETRY

Objective: Students will demonstrate their understanding of simple geometric shapes and equations.

Parent Tip: In this section, it is very important for your child to study the figures very carefully to get the information s/he needs. Once s/he has selected an answer, it would be wise for him/her to re-check his/her work.

Read each problem carefully and choose the correct answer.

EXAMPLE:

How many angles does the above figure have?

    a. 2
    b. 4
    c. 6
    d. 8

The correct answer is "b". The figure has four angles.

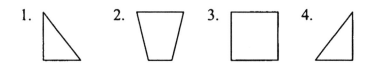

1. Which figures are congruent?

    a. 1 and 2
    b. 2 and 3
    c. 1 and 4
    d. none of the above

2. What is the name for the part of the circle shown by the dotted line?

   a. diameter
   b. radius
   c. circumference
   d. none of the above

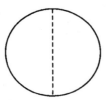

3. How many sides, or faces, does this figure have?

   a. 3
   b. 5
   c. 6
   d. 8

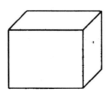

4. What is the area of this figure?

   a. 12 square inches
   b. 20 square inches
   c. 22 square inches
   d. none of the above

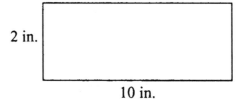

5. What is the pattern of the angles from A to C?

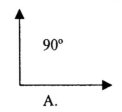 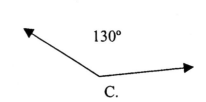

90° A.   40° B.   130° C.

   a. obtuse, acute, obtuse
   b. right, acute, obtuse
   c. right, acute, acute
   d. right, obtuse, obtuse

6. Which figure shows a line of symmetry?

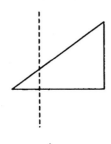 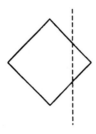 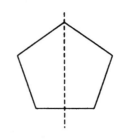 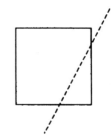

   A.   B.   C.   D.

7. In which pair are the lines probably parallel?

a.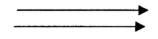

b.

c.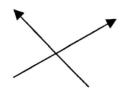

d.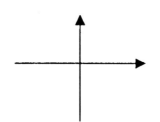

8. Which of these two figures are congruent?

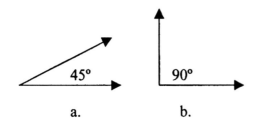 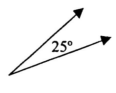 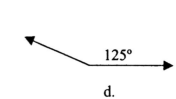

1.   2.   3.   4.

 a. 1,2
 b. 2,3
 c. 1,4
 d. none of the above

9. Which of the following is an obtuse angle?

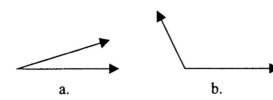 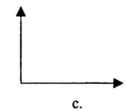 

  a.   b.   c.   d.

10. Which of these is a right angle?

  a.   b.   c.   d.

MATH
Answer Key

Problem Solving

1. b
2. a
3. d
4. b
5. a
6. b
7. c
8. d
9. d
10. b
11. c
12. c
13. d
14. c
15. c
16. c
17. b
18. b
19. b
20. c
21. b
22. b
23. c
24. a
25. c

Procedures

1. c
2. a
3. d
4. b
5. c
6. b
7. b
8. a
9. c
10. a
11. a
12. c
13. b
14. c
15. b
16. b
17. c
18. b
19. c
20. c
21. b
22. b
23. c
24. d
25. c
26. c
27. b
28. a
29. c
30. c
31. c
32. d
33. b
34. b
35. d

Concepts

1. c
2. b
3. c
4. d
5. c
6. a
7. b
8. c
9. d
10. c
11. b
12. d
13. b
14. b

Computation

1. b
2. c
3. d
4. a
5. c
6. b
7. a
8. c
9. a
10. b
11. b
12. a
13. d
14. c
15. c

Fractions & Decimals

1. c
2. a
3. c
4. b
5. b
6. d
7. b
8. a
9. b
10. a
11. d
12. b
13. c
14. d
15. a

Geometry

1. c
2. a
3. c
4. b
5. b
6. c
7. a
8. c
9. d
10. c

SOCIAL STUDIES

Content Cluster: UNITED STATES GEOGRAPHY

Objective: To identify and understand the significance of the major geographic features of the United States. Students will use maps to identify the political and physical features of the United States.

Parent Tip: This section of the test deals exclusively with United States geography. Your child should be quite familiar with the important political features (such as major cities), and physical features (such as rivers and mountain ranges), to do well on this section of the test.

Read the question and choose the correct answer.

EXAMPLE:

The only states that border Mexico and a major body of water are

a. Texas and Florida
b. California and Texas
c. Arizona and Texas
d. None of the above

The correct answer is "b". California borders Mexico and the Pacific Ocean, while Texas borders Mexico and the Gulf of Mexico.

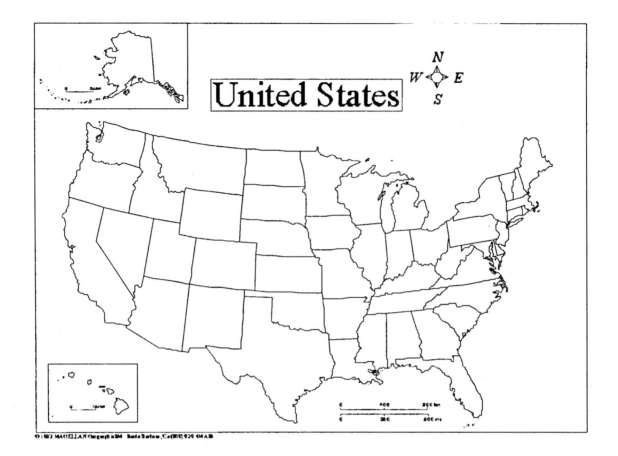

1. Which of the following states is not part of the Northeast Region?

   a. Rhode Island
   b. Pennsylvania
   c. New Jersey
   d. Georgia

2. The states of Illinois and Nebraska have all of the following in common EXCEPT

   a. both are agricultural states
   b. both are located in the Midwest
   c. both have approximately the same population
   d. both are made up of flat plains

3. In square miles, which region of the United States is the largest?

   a. The South
   b. The Midwest
   c. The Northeast
   d. The Far West

5th Grade Edition   66

4. Which major American river once formed the western border of the U.S.?

   a. the Delaware
   b. the Mississippi
   c. the Ohio
   d. the Missouri

5. The Northeastern region and the Southern region have all of the following in common EXCEPT

   a. both contain states that touch the Atlantic Ocean.
   b. both contain major population centers.
   c. both contain states that were part of the 13 colonies.
   d. both are closer to the equator than the North Pole.

6. Besides the Atlantic and the Pacific Ocean, what is the third Ocean that touches the United States?

   a. The Indian Ocean
   b. The Persian Gulf
   c. The Mediterranean Ocean
   d. The Gulf of Mexico

7. All of the following states are considered part of the Southern Region of the United States except

   a. Louisiana
   b. Mississippi
   c. North Dakota
   d. North Carolina

8. The states of California, New Mexico, and Texas have the following in common:

   a. All are in the Western region of the United States.
   b. All are closer to the equator than the North Pole.
   c. All were once part of Mexico.
   d. All of the above.

9. All of these statements about the Ohio River are true EXCEPT:

   a. The Ohio forms a northern border for Kentucky and West Virginia.
   b. The Ohio was once used as a "road" to transport goods from the frontier to foreign nations.
   c. The Ohio connects the Atlantic Ocean to the Mississippi River.
   d. The Ohio is one of the largest rivers in the United States.

10. Alaska and Hawaii have all of the following in common EXCEPT:

    a. They were admitted to the United States after 1945.
    b. They are not part of the continental United States.
    c. They have a similar climate.
    d. They are both popular vacation spots for Americans.

11. Place the three major mountain ranges in the United States in their proper order from west to east.

    a. Sierra Nevada, Appalachian, Rockies
    b. Sierra Nevada, Rockies, Appalachian
    c. Rockies, Appalachian, Sierra Nevada
    d. None of the above

12. Which of these states is NOT part of the Great Plains?

    a. North Dakota
    b. South Dakota
    c. Wisconsin
    d. Kansas

13. Alaska and Hawaii have the following things in common EXCEPT

    a. both are NOT part of the Continental United States.
    b. both touch the Atlantic Ocean.
    c. both were the last two states to join the United States.
    d. both states were once territories of foreign countries.

14. The Missouri River forms a border for which state?

    a. Indiana
    b. Florida
    c. Texas
    d. Arkansas

15. Which of the following states is not landlocked?

    a. Kansas
    b. Tennessee
    c. West Virginia
    d. Oregon

16. Which of the following states is regularly affected by hurricanes?

    a. Idaho
    b. Vermont
    c. Iowa
    d. Louisiana

17. Which of the following states are regularly affected by fierce winds and snow?

    a. Georgia
    b. Oklahoma
    c. Illinois
    d. Arizona

18. In terms of population, rank these states from most populated to least populated.

    a. Michigan, New York, Maine
    b. Maine, New York, Michigan
    c. New York, Maine, Michigan
    d. None of the above

19. All of the following states are considered part of New England except

    a. Massachusetts.
    b. Vermont.
    c. New Jersey.
    d. Connecticut.

20. What five states does the Pacific Ocean border?

    a. California, Oregon, Washington, Mexico, Alaska
    b. California, Oregon, Washington, Mexico, Hawaii
    c. California, Oregon, Washington, Alaska, Hawaii
    d. California, Oregon, Mexico, Alaska, Hawaii

Content Cluster: EARLY VOYAGES OF EXPLORERS OF THE AMERICAS.

Objective: Students will explain the motives and accomplishments of early explorers. Students will understand the obstacles faced by them.

Parent Tip: To do well on this section of the test, your child should be very familiar with the Spanish, English, and French voyages of discovery to the North American Continent in the 15th – 17th centuries.

Directions: Read the question and choose the correct answer.

EXAMPLE:

What do Christopher Columbus and Francis Drake have in common?

    a. Both sailed for England.
    b. Both sailed for Spain.
    c. Both became outcasts in their native lands.
    d. Both took Native Americans as slaves.

The correct answer here is "c". Both became outcasts in their native lands.

1. The voyage of Columbus from Palos, Spain to the West Indies in 1492 proved

    a. that Columbus had discovered the United States.
    b. that Columbus could treat Native Americans with respect.
    c. that Columbus would die a rich man.
    d. that Columbus' basic theory of navigation was correct.

2. Which of the following European explorers did not sail for Spain?

    a. Hernando de Soto
    b. Sir Francis Drake
    c. Hernano Cortez
    d. Francisco Pizarro

3. French Explorers such as Hudson and Cartier brought all of the following back from America except:

    a. beaver pelts.
    b. spices.
    c. gold.
    d. fish.

4. Which of the following was the first English colony in America?

    a. Roanoke, North Carolina
    b. Jamestown, Virginia
    c. Philadelphia, Pennsylvania
    d. Plymouth, Massachusetts

5. All of these differences between French and Spanish exploration of the Americas are true EXCEPT:

    a. French explorers sailed north toward Canada, while Spanish explorers sailed South toward Latin America.
    b. Spanish explorers were interested in dominating Native Americans, while the French were more interested in trading with them.
    c. Many important French explorers were foreign-born while Spain's key explorers were from Spain.
    d. Only Spanish explorers were interested in taking gold from Native Americans.

6. Among Henry Hudson's accomplishments was

    a. defeating the Spanish Armada
    b. stealing gold from Spanish ships
    c. giving the Dutch a claim to land in North America
    d. being knighted by Queen Elizabeth

7. Spanish conquistadors used all of the following to help them dominate Native Americans EXCEPT

    a. weaponry.
    b. the Catholic Church.
    c. a peace treaty with England.
    d. horses.

8. Which European Ruler was not involved in financing voyages of discovery?

   a. Queen Elizabeth I
   b. King Ferdinand
   c. Prince Henry the Navigator
   d. Queen Elizabeth II

9. The Northwest Passage was

   a. a legendary trade route.
   b. a secret way to get to Asia from America.
   c. never discovered.
   d. all of the above.

10. Sir Francis Drake was the first English explorer to

    a. befriend Spanish ships.
    b. discover California.
    c. circumnavigate the globe and visit California.
    d. Enrage Queen Elizabeth after he returned home.

11. Ponce de Leon, a Spanish explorer, spent his time in the New World searching for

    a. the Northwest Passage.
    b. the Fountain of Youth.
    c. the Ark of Covenant.
    d. buried treasure.

12. Spanish colonies were located in all of the following areas except:

    a. Mexico.
    b. the American Southwest.
    c. the American Midwest.
    d. South America.

13. French colonies were primarily located in

    a. New England.
    b. The Western states of America.
    c. Canada.
    d. Florida and the Caribbean.

14. French merchants came to the New World in search of

    a. beaver pelts.
    b. tobacco.
    c. corn and rice.
    d. all of the above

15. The most common hazard for a European sailor in the 16th and 17th centuries was

    a. shipwrecks.
    b. poor navigational techniques.
    c. diseases such as scurvy.
    d. injuries sustained in battle.

16. The reason more European nations did not undertake their own voyages was

    a. financing these trips was very expensive
    b. much of the New World was claimed already
    c. there weren't enough experienced sea captains
    d. all of the above

17. Cabeza de Vaca, a Spanish explorer, is best known for

    a. sailing with Cortez.
    b. sailing with Colombus.
    c. living among the Indians.
    d. none of the above

18. The French set up a series of trading posts along the

    a. Hudson River.
    b. St. Lawrence River.
    c. Atlantic coast.
    d. Mississippi River.

19. European explorers sailed for which reason?

    a. to spread Christianity
    b. to become famous
    c. to become wealthy
    d. all of the above

Content Cluster: LIFE IN THE AMERICAN COLONIES

Objective: Students will understand the geographic, political, economic and social differences and similarities in the regions of New England, the Mid-Atlantic Colonies, and the South.

> **Parent Tip:** To be successful in this section of the test, your child should be familiar with the Colonial period in American History that began in 1607 with the founding of Jamestown, and ended in 1775 with the outbreak of the American Revolution.

Directions: Read the question and choose the best answer.

EXAMPLE:

The reason the first English colony in Roanoke Island, North Carolina did not survive was:

a. The settlers were not prepared to stay.
b. The settlers were attacked by Native American tribes.
c. The settlers did not have adequate food supplies.
d. All of the above

The best answer is "d". Although no one knows exactly what happened to the "lost colony," most historians agree that all of the above contributed to the failure of the colony.

1. After leaving Virginia, Pocahontas sailed to England and married

a. John Smith.
b. John Rolfe.
c. Sir Walter Raleigh.
d. William Bradford.

2. The Puritans believed in a covenant between themselves and God. Which of the following words means the same as "covenant"?

a. prayer
b. assistance
c. help
d. agreement

3. All of the following statements about Puritan communities in New England are true except:

   a. Non-Puritans were welcome in these towns.
   b. Daily life was based on religion.
   c. Church services were called "meetings."
   d. Settlers didn't feel they could worship in England without persecution.

4. Quakers such as William Penn practiced a religious belief called tolerance. Which of the following terms means the same as "tolerance"?

   a. judgment
   b. prayer
   c. acceptance
   d. study

5. Most people in the 13 Colonies farmed for a living. If you were a farmer in the Southern Colonies, you might have planted any of the following crops EXCEPT

   a. tobacco.
   b. wheat.
   c. cotton.
   d. rice.

6. The Middle Colonies would have been the best region of America for growing crops because

   a. peace existed between colonists and Native Americans.
   b. the soil was very rich.
   c. crops could be sold along the rivers.
   d. all of the above

7. Regarding slaves and indentured servants,

   a. all indentured servants were poor people who signed work contracts.
   b. indentured servants would become free after a set time period.
   c. slaves worked primarily in the Southern Colonies.
   d. all of the above

8. The largest and most powerful American colony in the 17th and 18th centuries was

   a. New York.
   b. Virginia.
   c. Pennsylvania.
   d. Massachusetts.

9. Despite all of the problems at Jamestown, the colony survived because

   a. the Indian attacks suddenly stopped.
   b. tobacco was discovered as an export crop.
   c. wheat was discovered as an export crop.
   d. strong religious affiliations existed in the colony.

10. All of the following statements are true about all 13 original American colonies in 1770 EXCEPT

   a. many people still thought of themselves as British.
   b. most people made their living by farming.
   c. there was little equality between men and women.
   d. many people wanted a war with England.

11. In 1621 the pilgrims were taught basic hunting and farming skills by

   a. Chief Powhatan.
   b. Pocahontas.
   c. Squanto.
   d. Crazy Horse.

12. The Middle Colonies include:

   a. South Carolina, Georgia, Virginia, and North Carolina.
   b. Rhode Island, New Hampshire, Massachusetts, and Connecticut.
   c. New York, Pennsylvania, New Jersey, Delaware, and Maryland.
   d. All of the above

13. One main difference between Southern and Middle colony farms was:

   a. Southern colony farms grew food primarily for export, while Middle colony farms grew food to eat.
   b. Southern colony farms grew food primarily to eat, while Middle colony farms grew food to export.
   c. Crops in Southern colony farms were grown primarily by slaves, while Middle colony farms had no slaves.
   d. Crops in Middle colony farms were grown primarily by slaves, while Southern colony farms had no slaves.

Content Cluster: THE AMERICAN REVOLUTION

Objective: Students will understand the course, effects, and human consequences of the War for Independence.

> **Parent Tip:** To do well in this section of the test, your child should be very familiar with the key people, places, and events of the American War for Independence.

Directions: Read the question and choose the best answer.

EXAMPLE:

The Continental Army's first major victory of the war took place in:

a. Yorktown, Virginia
b. Philadelphia, Pennsylvania
c. Trenton, New Jersey
d. Lexington, Massachusetts

The correct answer is "c". Washington's daring midnight crossing of the Delaware River before the Battle of Trenton secured the Army's first major victory of the war.

Josephine is writing a research paper on the American Revolution. Here is her outline Please review it carefully, since you will need this information to answer questions 1 – 3.

THE AMERICAN REVOLUTION

I.   Causes of the conflict with England

A. The French – Indian War
B.
C. The Sons of Liberty/Tax Protests
D. The Boston Massacre

II.   The fighting begins

A. Paul Revere's Ride – April 19th, 1775
B. The Battle of Lexington – April 19th, 1775
C.

III.

    A. Continental Congress – June/July 1776
    B. Committee of Five
    C. Thomas Jefferson Drafts the Document
    D. Celebrations Across the Colonies on July 4th

1. Which of the following belongs in Section I of the outline?

    a. The U.S. Constitution
    b. George Washington
    c. The Stamp Act
    d. The Battle of Yorktown

2. Which of the following belongs in Section II of the outline?

    a. The Battle of Trenton
    b. The Battle of Saratoga
    c. The Battle of Breed's Hill
    d. The Battle of Concord

3. Which of the following titles belongs as the heading for section III of the outline?

    a. After the Declaration was Written
    b. The Declaration of Independence
    c. Jefferson Writes the Declaration
    d. Reasons the Declaration Was Written

4. The Battle of Concord showed the British army that

    a. Americans could be aggressive in battle.
    b. Americans would use their knowledge of the natural landscape to shoot British soldiers.
    c. American volunteers would fight to defend their lands just like professional soldiers.
    d. All of the above

5. General George Washington's first victory came at the battle of

    a. Trenton.
    b. Cowpens.
    c. Breed's Hill.
    d. Yorktown.

6. The largest killer of American soldiers during the War for Independence was

   a. British bullets.
   b. Smallpox.
   c. British bayonets.
   d. British cannons.

7. The Battle of Breed's Hill in June of 1775 was fought near what major city?

   a. Boston
   b. New York
   c. Philadelphia
   d. Williamsburg

8. The Continental Army crossed the Delaware on Christmas night, 1776, before which major battle?

   a. Yorktown
   b. Trenton
   c. Princeton
   d. Monmoth

9. Which of the following key military leaders was NOT involved in the Battle of Yorktown in 1781?

   a. George Washington
   b. Lord Cornwalis
   c. Marquis de Lafayette
   d. General John Burgoyne

10. Deborah Sampson served during the Revolution by

   a. dressing as a man and going into battle.
   b. tending a cannon during the Battle of Monmoth.
   c. nursing sick soldiers at Valley Forge.
   d. sewing the original American flag for General Washington.

Content Cluster: FOUNDATIONS OF THE AMERICAN REPUBLIC

Objective: Students will analyze the important ideas that form the foundation of the American Republic.

Parent Tip: This section of the test deals with the ideological foundations of our government that are found in such documents as the Constitution and the Declaration of Independence. To be successful on this section of the test, your child will need to be familiar with these documents and will need to be able to analyze their meanings.

Directions: Read the question and choose the best answer.

EXAMPLE:

The man called the "father of the Constitution" is:

a. George Washington
b. James Madison
c. Thomas Jefferson
d. None of the above

The correct answer is "b". James Madison was the chief architect of the Constitution.

Excerpt from the Declaration of Independence

In Congress, July 4th, 1776

The Unanimous Declaration of the Thirteen United States of America

When in the course of human events, it becomes necessary for one people to dissolve the political bands which have connected them with another, and to assume among Powers of the earth, the separate and equal station to which the Laws of Nature and of Nature's God entitle them, a decent respect to the opinions of mankind requires that they should declare the causes which impel them the separation.

1. Who was the main author of this document?

a. Thomas Paine
b. Thomas Jefferson
c. John Adams
d. Benjamin Franklin

2. In the first sentence, the work "dissolve" probably means

   a. break.
   b. disappear.
   c. strengthen.
   d. examine.

3. The main idea behind this first paragraph could be summarized as:

   a. America wants independence immediately.
   b. America wants to strengthen ties to other nations.
   c. America doesn't have to explain why it wants freedom.
   d. God has given Americans the right to be independent.

4. The author has capitalized the words "Powers" and "Nature's God" to let you know that

   a. those words are especially important.
   b. those words refer to the power given by God.
   c. those words show that America can act alone.
   d. those words prove America's own power in the world.

5. The words "connected them with another" refer to the fact that

   a. America is a part of England.
   b. America was part of England, but no longer.
   c. America was part of many European nations.
   d. All of the above

6. After reading the first paragraph, what do you think is coming next in the document?

   a. more talk about America's independence
   b. a list of reasons for Americans to seek independence
   c. more talk about why America should stay connected to England
   d. all of the above

7. Why is the word "unanimous" important in the document?

   a. It shows that the states didn't want to be recognized for seeking independence.
   b. It showed England that all of America was united.
   c. It showed that there were disagreements between states.
   d. all of the above

8. What was the response of King George III and his Parliament to this Declaration?

  a. They immediately gave America its independence.
  b. They stopped the war with America.
  c. They ignored it and continued to send British troops to America.
  d. They asked France to help them crush the rebellion in America.

9. One important idea that Jefferson was forced to take out of the Declaration was

  a. asking that women be allowed to vote.
  b. asking that indentured servitude be stopped.
  c. asking that slavery be ended in America.
  d. asking that America expand to the Mississippi River.

10. This document was created in what American city?

  a. New York City
  b. Philadelphia
  c. Boston
  d. Charlestown

The Preamble of the United States Constitution

"We the People of the United States, in order to form a more perfect Union, establish Justice, insure domestic Tranquility, provide for the common defence, promote the general Welfare, and secure the Blessings of Liberty to ourselves and our Posterity, do ordain and establish this Constitution for the United States of America."

11. The word "preamble" probably means

  a. the last passage of the document.
  b. the words before the document.
  c. the most important part of the document.
  d. the most interesting part of the document.

12. The United States Constitution was written in:

  a. New York in 1777.
  b. Boston in 1778.
  c. Philadelphia in 1787.
  d. None of the above

13. The Constitution was written because

    a. The current United States Government had failed.
    b. The American Revolution had ended.
    c. The British forced America to create it.
    d. All of the above

14. The words "insure domestic Tranquility" probably means

    a. stopping wars against other nations.
    b. making all citizens rich.
    c. creating peace and happiness in America.
    d. ending the American Revolution.

15. How might America "provide for the common defence?"

    a. Educate children
    b. collect food
    c. end state militias
    d. all of the above

16. What could be meant by the "Blessings of Liberty"?

    a. peace
    b. freedom
    c. happiness
    d. all of the above

17. What could be meant by the word "Posterity"?

    a. people living after we do
    b. friends
    c. children in our homes
    d. neighbors

18. All of the following founders of the United States attended the Constitutional Convention except:

    a. George Washington
    b. Thomas Jefferson
    c. Benjamin Franklin
    d. James Madison

SOCIAL STUDIES
Answer Key

US Geography

1. d
2. c
3. d
4. b
5. d
6. d
7. c
8. d
9. c
10. c
11. b
12. c
13. b
14. a
15. d
16. d
17. c
18. d
19. c
20. c

Early Voyages of Explorers

1. d
2. b
3. c
4. a
5. d
6. c
7. c
8. d

9. d
10. c
11. b
12. c
13. c
14. a
15. c
16. d
17. c
18. b
19. d

American Colonies

1. b
2. d
3. a
4. c
5. b
6. d
7. d
8. b
9. b
10. d
11. c
12. c
13. a

American Revolution

1. c
2. d
3. b
4. d

5. a
6. b
7. a
8. b
9. d
10. a

American Republic

1. b
2. a
3. d
4. b
5. b
6. b
7. b
8. c
9. c
10. b
11. b
12. c
13. a
14. c
15. c
16. d
17. a
18. b

SCIENCE

Content Cluster: EARTH SCIENCE

Objective: Students will understand basic scientific processes and facts related to weather, the water cycle, and basic astronomy.

> **Parent Tip:** These questions are based on the California Science Standards for 5th graders. Your child should have some familiarity with the topics covered on this section of the test. It is important that your child answer all the questions possible first so as not to waste valuable time on questions that may be too difficult or unfamiliar. If time permits, encourage your child to go back over any questions left blank.

Read the question and choose the correct answer.

EXAMPLE:

The hottest stars in our galaxy are _____ in color.

    a. blue
    b. red
    c. yellow
    d. none of the above

The correct answer is "a". The hottest stars in our galaxy are blue in color.

1. What is unique about Earth among all planets in our solar system?

    a. It is the only planet that contains water.
    b. It is the only planet that has ever had multi-cellular life as far as we know.
    c. It has the best conditions to support life.
    d. It is the only planet to revolve around the Sun.

2. The Sun is considered a

    a. star.
    b. planet.
    c. comet.
    d. asteroid.

3. The earth moves on it's own axis. This creates day and night and is called

    a. rotation.
    b. gravity.
    c. revolving.
    d. central force.

4. Jupiter and Saturn have the following things in common EXCEPT

    a. Neither planet is made of solid matter.
    b. Both planets have moons.
    c. Both planets are covered by poison gasses.
    d. Both planets have a red storm system at their center.

5. The conditions on Pluto would not support life because

    a. Pluto is too cold for living things to grow.
    b. Pluto is too small to support life.
    c. Pluto is not made of solid material.
    d. Pluto is not part of our Solar System.

6. The conditions on Mercury would not support life because:

    a. Mercury is not a planet.
    b. Mercury does not revolve around the Sun.
    c. Mercury is too hot to support life.
    d. Mercury is closest to the Sun.

7. Like other stars, the sun is a giant ball of hot _____.

    a. lava
    b. vapor
    c. gas
    d. none of the above

8. The two planets that have the most moons are

    a. Uranus and Neptune.
    b. Jupiter and Saturn.
    c. Neptune and Uranus.
    d. Earth and Mars.

9. Every _____, the earth rotates on it's own axis. It takes a _____ for the earth to revolve around the sun.

    a. year, day
    b. day, year
    c. year, month
    d. day, month

10. Even though comets look like fireballs, they are actually made of _____.

    a. rock
    b. gas
    c. oxygen
    d. ice

11. The average ocean depth is approximately

    a. 1 mile.
    b. 3 miles.
    c. 2 miles.
    d. none of the above

12. The size of an ocean wave depends upon

    a. the depth of the ocean or sea.
    b. the distance from shore.
    c. the strength and duration of wind.
    d. all of the above

13. The rise and fall of oceans, called tides, occur how often each day?

    a. twice
    b. once
    c. three times
    d. more than three times

14. The words *source*, *mouth*, and *banks* are all related to which bodies of water?

    a. streams
    b. rivers
    c. lakes
    d. seas

15. Approximately what percentage of the Earth's surface do glaciers currently cover?

    a. 3%
    b. 8%
    c. 5%
    d. 6%

16. Which layer of the earth do humans actually live on?

    a. core
    b. crust
    c. mantle
    d. none of the above

17. What is it that keeps humans from ascending too high above the earth's surface?

    a. electromagnetic forces
    b. limited technology
    c. atmospheric pressure
    d. the structure of the earth

18. Cold fronts and warm fronts refer to

    a. winds.
    b. weather changes.
    c. temperature changes.
    d. all of the above

19. Which layer of the atmosphere is the closest to the ground?

    a. exosphere
    b. stratosphere
    c. troposphere
    d. mesosphere

20. Dew, hail, sleet, and snow are all examples of

    a. moisture.
    b. precipitation.
    c. cold weather patterns.
    d. all of the above

21. A strong, rotating column of air reaching from a cloud to the ground is called a:

   a. hurricane
   b. thunderstorm
   c. tornado
   d. typhoon

22. The earth has areas of ice, such as the poles, and areas of intense heat. How can this be explained?

   a. The sun does not heat the earth evenly.
   b. The amount of heat given by the sun depends on the rotation of the earth.
   c. The warmer areas of the earth face the sun directly.
   d. All of the above

23. Scientists call all the land on Earth the

   a. atmosphere.
   b. lithosphere.
   c. biosphere.
   d. hydrosphere.

24. The equator is an imaginary line around Earth that divides Earth into two:

   a. stratospheres
   b. atmospheres
   c. hemispheres
   d. biospheres

25. The oxygen that you breathe is found in what great sphere that makes up planet Earth?

   a. atmosphere
   b. stratosphere
   c. lithosphere
   d. hemisphere

26. What layer of gas in the Earth's atmosphere absorbs most of the harmful ultraviolet radiation from the sun?

   a. ammonia
   b. hydrogen
   c. methane
   d. ozone

27. What is the most abundant gas in the atmosphere?

    a. oxygen
    b. carbon dioxide
    c. nitrogen
    d. hydrogen

28. What gas is used directly from the atmosphere by most plants and animals as an essential part of respiration?

    a. oxygen
    b. carbon dioxide
    c. nitrogen
    d. hydrogen

29. Which of the four main layers of the atmosphere is furthest from Earth?

    a. stratosphere
    b. thermosphere
    c. troposphere
    d. mesosphere

30. A meteor, also known as a _____, is a streak of _____that is produced by the vaporization of interplanetary particles as they enter the Earth's atmosphere.

    a. comet/debris
    b. shooting star or falling star/light
    c. constellation/dust
    d. rock/vapor

31. What is the largest ocean on Earth?

    a. Atlantic
    b. Pacific
    c. Indian
    d. Arctic

32. What term do oceanographers use to describe the amount of dissolved salts in ocean water?

    a. Alkalinity
    b. Salinity
    c. Carbon
    d. Chlorine

33. What is the ocean zone where waves and currents mix the water?

    a. deep zone
    b. drop zone
    c. surface zone
    d. current zone

34. What effect occurs when carbon dioxide and other gases in the atmosphere absorb the infrared rays, forming a kind of "heat blanket" around the Earth?

    a. greenhouse
    b. grayhouse
    c. tollhouse
    d. sunhouse

35. Air pressure is measured with an instrument called a

    a. thermometer.
    b. anemometer.
    c. microscope.
    d. barometer.

36. Water that falls from the atmosphere to the Earth is called

    a. vapor.
    b. crystals.
    c. precipitation.
    d. wind.

37. A wind that blows more often from one direction than from any other direction is called a _____ wind.

    a. strong
    b. prevailing
    c. weak
    d. cold

38. The United States has six major climate regions. Scientists classify areas with similar climates, plants, and animals into divisions called _____.

    a. biomes
    b. regions
    c. environments
    d. space

Content Cluster: PHYSICAL SCIENCE

Objective: Students will understand basic scientific ideas related to the study of matter.

Parent Tip: Elements and their combinations account for all the varied types of matter in the world. Your child should have the basic understanding of the everyday substances such as solids, liquids and gasses, and their chemical compositions.

EXAMPLE:

What is the scientific name for water?

    a. He
    b. H_2O
    c. O_2
    d. CO_2

The correct answer is "b". The scientific name for water is H_2O.

Read the question and choose the correct answer.

1. The amount of space something takes up is called its _____.

    a. weight
    b. mass
    c. volume
    d. height

2. Which of the following is NOT a state of matter?

    a. solid
    b. gas
    c. liquid
    d. vapor

3. Density describes the mass of an object divided by its _____.

    a. volume
    b. height
    c. weight
    d. none of the above

4. Protons, neutrons, and electrons are all considered _____.

    a. tiny parts of matter
    b. subatomic particles
    c. too small to be seen
    d. all of the above

5. Protons, neutrons, and electrons combine to form a/n _____.

    a. atom
    b. molecule
    c. quark
    d. none of the above

6. When atoms join together to form molecules made up of different elements, this is called _____.

    a. state of matter
    b. change of matter
    c. compound
    d. none of the above

7. All living organisms must contain which element?

    a. hydrogen
    b. carbon
    c. glycerin
    d. none of the above

8. Which of the following substances is NOT an acid?

    a. battery acid
    b. orange
    c. apple juice
    d. soap

9. All of the following are examples of solid matter EXCEPT:

    a. rocks
    b. oil
    c. trees
    d. glass

10. Which of the following substances can transform into a solid, liquid, or a gas?

   a. blood
   b. metal
   c. water
   d. none of the above

11. The chemical compound CO_2 is another name for

   a. water.
   b. carbon dioxide.
   c. carbon monoxide.
   d. nitrogen dioxide.

12. The main difference between protons and neutrons is _____.

   a. protons are positively charged; neutrons are not
   b. only neutrons can be seen with the human eye
   c. protons are heavier than neutrons
   d. only neutrons are found inside the nucleus of an atom

13. Which of the four elements listed is the heaviest?

   a. helium
   b. hydrogen
   c. oxygen
   d. uranium

14. The lightest element in the periodic table is _____.

   a. helium
   b. hydrogen
   c. oxygen
   d. uranium

15. The air we breathe is made up mostly of _____.

   a. nitrogen
   b. hydrogen
   c. argon
   d. carbon dioxide

16. Bases are chemical compounds that contain the elements of _____ and _____ mixed together.

    a. hydrogen and iron
    b. oxygen and sodium
    c. hydrogen and oxygen
    d. none of the above

17. You see and touch hundreds of things every day. Although most of these things differ from one another, they all share one important quality: They are all forms of

    a. life.
    b. heat.
    c. matter.
    d. property.

18. What is the resistance of an object to change in its motion?

    a. inertia
    b. speed
    c. force
    d. effect

19. The properties of mass and volume can be used to describe another important general property that is the mass per unit volume of an object.

    a. mass
    b. density
    c. volume
    d. weight

20. A pencil, a cube of sugar, a metal coin, and an ice cream cone are examples of

    a. solids.
    b. liquids.
    c. properties.
    d. mass.

21. If you could examine the internal structure of many solids, you would see that the particles making up the solids are arranged in a regular repeating pattern called a

    a. metal.
    b. gas.
    c. crystal.
    d. liquid.

22. What is the change of a solid to a liquid?

    a. burning
    b. freezing
    c. heating
    d. melting

23. The temperature at which a substance changes from a liquid to a solid is called its

    a. freezing point.
    b. burning point.
    c. boiling point.
    d. heating point.

24. If a substance in the gas phase loses heat energy, it changes into a liquid. Scientists call this change in phase

    a. precipitation.
    b. melting.
    c. freezing.
    d. condensation.

25. The change of a substance from a liquid to a gas is called

    a. evaporation.
    b. vaporization.
    c. freezing.
    d. condensation.

26. Another name for a chemical change is a

    a. chemical difference.
    b. chemical force.
    c. chemical reaction.
    d. chemical property.

27. What is matter that consists of two or more substances mixed together but not chemically combined?

    a. solution
    b. combination
    c. mixture
    d. sample

28. A substance that dissolves in water is said to be

    a. soluble.
    b. mixed.
    c. blended.
    d. wet.

29. What do you call a compound that is made of two or more atoms chemically bonded together?

    a. factor
    b. chemical
    c. element
    d. molecule

30. The number of protons in the nucleus of an atom is called the

    a. atomic batch.
    b. atomic number.
    c. mass number.
    d. atomic mass.

31. What force causes apples to fall from a tree and planets to remain in orbit around the sun?

    a. strong force
    b. weak force
    c. gravity
    d. critical force

32. What is a physical property of metal?

    a. luster
    b. ductility
    c. malleability
    d. all of the above

33. Because they tend to lose electrons, most metals will react chemically with water or with elements in the atmosphere. Such a chemical reaction often results in

    a. rotting.
    b. melting.
    c. corrosion.
    d. exploding.

Content Cluster: LIFE SCIENCE

Objective: Students will understand key systems such as respiration, reproduction and digestion used by both plant and animal species.

Parent Tip: This section of the test deals with basic biological properties of plants and animals. Your child should have an understanding of plant and animal systems includes the reproductive, circulatory and digestive systems. This area also focuses on photosynthesis.

EXAMPLE:

Plants and animal cells break down _____ to obtain energy.

a. air
b. water
c. sugar
d. solid foods

The correct answer is "c". Plants and animal cells break down sugar to obtain energy.

Read the question and choose the correct answer.

1. Which of the following statements are true about mammal reproduction?

a. In mammals, eggs develop inside the mother's body.
b. In mammals, babies are born live.
c. In mammals, babies are cared for after birth.
d. all of the above

2. The process that some insects go through to completely change their body and appearance is called

a. reproduction.
b. fragmentation.
c. metamorphosis.
d. none of the above

3. How do fish reproduce?

   a. fermentation
   b. laying eggs
   c. fragmentation
   d. none of the above

4. Which of these statements about fish is untrue?

   a. All fish have gills.
   b. All fish have backbones.
   c. All fish have scaly skin.
   d. All fish have bone skeletons.

5. Which of the following animals would be considered an amphibian?

   a. monkey
   b. tortoise
   c. salamander
   d. komodo dragon

6. Mammals that have underdeveloped babies and then place them inside a pouch to continue growing are called _____.

   a. monotremes
   b. marsupials
   c. placental mammals
   d. none of the above

7. Most human beings would be considered _____.

   a. herbivores
   b. omnivores
   c. carnivores
   d. all of the above

8. The scientific name for plants that produce exposed seeds is _____.

   a. angiosperms
   b. dicots
   c. gymnosperms
   d. none of the above

9. Which of the following plants does not belong in the seed plant category?

    a. roses
    b. tomatoes
    c. spruce tree
    d. ferns

10. The process by which a plant's chlorophyll captures energy from the sun is called

    a. photosynthesis.
    b. transportation.
    c. conduction.
    d. none of the above

11. Which of the following statements about roots is true?

    a. Roots anchor plants into the ground.
    b. Roots absorb water from the ground.
    c. Roots store materials needed by the plant.
    d. all of the above

12. Most plants reproduce through _____.

    a. reproduction
    b. seeds
    c. pollination
    d. fertilization

13. Which of the following is not part of a flower?

    a. petal
    b. root
    c. stamen
    d. anther

14. Seedless plants, such as ferns, reproduce by _____.

    a. pollination
    b. fertilization
    c. spores
    d. vegetative reproduction

15. In addition to sunlight and chlorophyll, a green plant needs carbon dioxide and water to perform photosynthesis. Carbon dioxide is a gas found in the atmosphere. It enters the plant through openings on the surface of the leaf called

    a. pore.
    b. crack.
    c. stomata.
    d. connection.

16. Animals obtain food by eating green plants or by eating other animals that eat green plants. Organisms that cannot produce their own food and thus must eat other organisms to obtain energy are called

    a. autotrophs.
    b. heterotrophs.
    c. mesotrophs.
    d. mendotrophs.

17. _____ is a process in which simple food substances such as glucose are broken down, and the energy they contain is released.

    a. Aspiration
    b. Ventilation
    c. Respiration
    d. Bleeding

18. Which system delivers food and oxygen to body cells and carries carbon dioxide and other waste products away from body cells?

    a. digestive
    b. respiratory
    c. musculatory
    d. circulatory

19. In the circulatory system, blood moves from the _____ to the lungs and back to the _____. Blood then travels to all the cells of the body and returns again.

    a. brain
    b. heart
    c. stomach
    d. liver

20. What is the largest blood vessel in the body?

    a. vena cava
    b. ventricle
    c. vein
    d. aorta

21. What are extremely thin-walled blood vessels called?

    a. veins
    b. arteries
    c. ventricles
    d. capillaries

22. What blood vessels carry blood back to the heart?

    a. veins
    b. arteries
    c. ventricles
    d. capillaries

23. What are the most numerous cells in the blood?

    a. white blood cells
    b. yellow blood cells
    c. red blood cells
    d. thick cells

24. What are the nutrients that are used to build and repair body parts called?

    a. acids
    b. proteins
    c. carbohydrates
    d. none of the above

25. In addition to proteins, carbohydrates, and fats, your body also needs
    _____ and _____.

    a. vitamins and vegetables
    b. minerals and vegetables
    c. vitamins and minerals
    d. vitamins and bacteria

SCIENCE
Answer Key

Earth Science

1. c
2. a
3. a
4. d
5. a
6. c
7. c
8. b
9. b
10. d
11. c
12. d
13. a
14. b
15. a
16. b
17. c
18. d
19. c
20. d
21. c
22. d
23. b
24. c
25. a
26. d
27. c
28. a
29. b
30. d
31. b
32. b
33. c

34. a
35. d
36. c
37. b
38. a

Physical Science

1. c
2. d
3. a
4. d
5. a
6. c
7. b
8. d
9. b
10. c
11. b
12. a
13. d
14. b
15. a
16. c
17. c
18. a
19. b
20. a
21. c
22. d
23. a
24. d
25. b
26. c
27. c

28. a
29. d
30. b
31. c
32. d
33. c

Life Science

1. d
2. c
3. b
4. d
5. c
6. b
7. b
8. c
9. d
10. a
11. d
12. b
13. b
14. c
15. c
16. b
17. c
18. d
19. b
20. d
21. d
22. a
23. c
24. b
25. c

NOTES